The Way of the Image
The Orientational Approach to the Psyche

by

Yoram Kaufmann

Copyright © 2009 Yoram Kaufmann

All rights reserved. No part of this book may be reproduced or transmitted in any form or by any means, electronic or mechanical, including photocopying, recording, or by information storage and retrieval systems, without the written permission of the publisher, except by a reviewer who may quote brief passages in a review.

The essays "The Way of the Image" and "Angels" previously appeared in monographs by the Assisi Foundation, Brattleboro, Vermont.

Printed in the United States of America

ISBN-13: 978-1-935184-00-3

Library of Congress Control Number: 2009927629

Cover art: Rogue VI Illustrations © Eric J. Heller 2005

Published by Zahav Books Inc. New York, New York
Contact: info@zahavbooks.com

Contents

The Way of the Image 1
   The Orientational Approach to the Psyche

The Way of the Image II 25
   What Do I Say (or Don't Say)
   An Orientational Approach to Therapeutic Technique

The Analyst of My Dreams 35

Angels 53

The Dreams of Gilgamesh as a Mythic Layer
   of the Psyche 59

   Notes and Sources 73

About the Author 75

Preface

This volume is the culmination and distillation of close to 50 years of working with people, through the twists and turns of a career that started with my serving as a volunteer in a free walk-in clinic for adolescents in 1960, to private practice in 1972, and simultaneously teaching for more than 25 years in the C.G. Jung Institute in New York. It was there that my ideas slowly took shape and coalesced, first in theoretical courses and in clinical case-seminars, and finally articulated in public when I was invited to lecture at the Vermont-Assisi conferences in 1996, at the invitation of Michael Conforti, to whom I owe a great debt of gratitude for enthusiastically encouraging me to come forward with my ideas. The segment on Gilgamesh originated in a talk I gave to the Round Table group in 1994. The Round Table Press kindly transcribed the talk, and Dolores O'Brien edited my remarks into an elegant form which the Press published in their journal **Review** (March/April 1996, Vol. 3, No. 4).

The book is dedicated to my parents, Lina (née Rochlin) and Herbert-Zvi, who did not get to see it, and to my wife, Rise, who has.

Y.K.

Introductory Comments

ELI WIESEL ONCE COMMENTED THAT WITH THE EMERGENCE OF THE RATIONAL MIND came the capacity to rationalize anything and everything. This is all too evident in our daily lives, where personal values, morality, and ethics are as mercurial as the sea, and meaning is laid upon a Procrustean bed, forced to conform to our personal needs. For all these reasons, we need to once again find a perspective that sees beyond the limitations of the conscious mind, listens to the whisperings of the soul, and strives to live in accordance to values inherent within the transcendent. Such is the legacy of the sages, and such is the opportunity afforded by this foray into the originality and brilliance of Dr. Yoram Kaufmann's work. His is a fresh, strong voice amid a sea of wavering opinions. His guidance and wisdom come from a long life lived in accordance with the mandates of the Self, not the capricious whims of the ego. His contributions will merit inclusion in the rich heritage of the Wisdom traditions.

After almost 30 years of clinical practice, I am more convinced than ever that life is shaped by influences far from our awareness. The blossoming of an exquisite orchid is guided by its innate sentience, yet the plant requires nurturing by someone who understands its specific needs and how *it* wants to grow, in order to assist in the expression of the orchid's intrinsic beauty.

I am often taken by the designs and patterns found in the natural world. If we look at trees along a shoreline, we begin to see how their shapes and contours are living testaments of their experience. Bent like an old man supported by his cane, the trees and their environment have become one. Their history is revealed by their shape, and their shape tells a story—that is for eyes and ears that are open, that are interested to hear.

So much of our dealings with the outer world, personal relationships, and even the human psyche, have become more a story of human survival than truth telling. We survive by spinning good enough meanings about our parents, families, our relationships and even our own behavior. We find convenient truths, tailor-made to store our experiences, all designed to keep us afloat, to maintain the life we have created. Fortunately, however, there is a truth greater than our personal renderings, a meaning extrinsic to what we want to believe, which affects us in profound ways.

So much of modern thought, including the practice of psychotherapy, promotes subjectivity as the panacea for all that ails. Perhaps when we open some time capsule 50 years from now, the voice of a therapist will be heard asking with the greatest of sincerity, "How do YOU feel?" and "What does that mean to YOU?" As patients, we are encouraged to talk about our feelings, our wishes, our thoughts. We are like Arachne weaving intricate designs about a life of which we know so little. Even Jungian psychology, which for so many years offered a needed refuge in its recognition of the soul and spirit, now in its search for modernity finds itself not only in newer clothes, but also echoing the sentiments of an all too secular world.

Now virtually lost and eclipsed are the values of the soul, and the wisdom of the elders who understood that modernity was but a piece of the fabric of a much deeper, richer life. **Eternity expressed in the temporal!** The elders and wise ones knew that answers to life's greatest questions exist within the soul, and it is there that we must go in order to learn about life.

Modern culture and contemporary psychology have stumbled in their attempts to find meaning, and to steady themselves grasp anything close at hand. Our collective answer is to adhere to the familiar environs of the conscious mind. Here we find comfort in memories and opinions that fit like a comfortable pair of shoes. However, mythology and the world's greatest spiritual traditions all speak of healing and the work of finding truth as a journey into unfamiliar terrain.

Jung, in his most formative years, traveled to Africa and to the American Southwest to see life as it once was, relatively untouched by the passage of time. In Africa he found the soul of man not only very much alive, but still revered by the people. This was in stark contrast to his experiences of European culture, where the important and needed advances of the rational mind all but eclipsed the richness of the world's spiritual traditions.

With the mind of a scientist, and eye of a visionary, Dr. Kaufmann's work takes us into the heart of the soul, wherein lies a meaning far greater than anything we can ever construct with our minds. Dr. Kaufmann's brilliance is evident throughout this book, as he teaches us to see the archetypal (non-subjectively derived) meaning of an image. He shows us the limitations of an interpretative approach, which seeks to understand by way of constructed meanings. Instead, he offers a truly novel way of working with images, which seeks to *translate* rather than *interpret*. Imagine receiving a letter in a foreign language containing important information about an upcoming meeting. Our task is to **translate**, not interpret, this material so that we can respond in a meaningful and appropriate way to its message. So too with material from the Objective Psyche, whose meaning needs to be translated and integrated into our life.

Dr. Kaufmann's **Orientational Approach** looks to the core, ontological significance of an image. In this regard, feelings, associations and reveries evoked by an image are not seen as descriptive or revelatory, but represent the individual's relationship and alignment to it. Central to the Orientational Approach is the art of discerning the archetypal dimension of an image, which when understood provides a point of reference to the individual's life situation.

Nature provides its own orientations. Perceived as a carefully crafted mosaic, New England apple trees pregnant with fruit, tomato having produced their gifts, and crisp evenings, evoke images of the approach of autumn. The growing season is ending, and we now can hopefully enjoy the fruits of our labors. Just as the arrival of fall brings with it a unique set of chores and activities, so too does the arrival of the autumn of one's life. Here we can begin to see the intrinsic relationship between external events, and how these eternal, cyclical patterns occurring in nature capture and express the rhythms of an individual life as well. Both are expressions of a natural, archetypal order. Dr. Kaufmann's work allows us to understand that every image, like every season, carries a set of innate, natural initiatives and mandates, all calling for inclusion within the individual psyche.

Jung often remarked that our human tendency is to make meaning of images. However, he added that our imperative is not to create meaning, but rather to discover the innate meaning inherent in a situation, as for instance, entering the autumn of life. Each image captures a unique, archetypal and vital reality with its own needs, proclivities, and tendencies. Dr. Kaufmann extends Jung's idea by encouraging us to enter the field of the image, to know it in its own right—to know its domain, needs, and tendencies. In entering the world of the archetype through its images, we allow the ego its due, while realizing that deeper meaning will only emerge as we have access to the transpersonal. Here we see how Dr. Kaufmann's work provides a truly spiritual approach to life, exemplifying that it is not the ego that dominates and informs, but the Self. The ego instead functions as translator, a midwife and a scribe for the Self, finding ways to integrate these specific messages into our lives.

Yoram Kaufmann belongs to the oral tradition of the "wise ones." He rarely ventures out to teach, eschews public attention, and continues in relative anonymity with his life and work. Dr. Kaufmann's privacy may suddenly be challenged as his work gains even greater recognition. Despite his private nature, his work has already influenced thousands of clinicians, scholars, and interested laypersons from around the world. Within the Assisi Institute Community, he is affectionately thought of as the *Compadre*, the Godfather, in recognition of the fundamental importance of his ideas to the evolution and development of the field of Archetypal Pattern Analysis. Dr. Kaufmann may not yet realize the many ways that this next generation has already taken his ideas into domains as diverse as psychotherapy, organizational consultation, the cinema, and international relations, and the lasting legacy his body of work will be for generations yet to follow.

It is a joy and privilege to be a friend, colleague, and student of Dr. Kaufmann, and I am delighted that his work will now receive even wider readership. He is a wise and eloquent man, with a unique approach to the Self and The Objective

Unconscious. I truly hope that his ideas stir you as much as they have me for the past 30 years, and provide for you a glimpse into the workings of the psyche.

His soul is reflected by his home, which is filled with magnificent orchids.

Michael Conforti
Brattleboro, Vermont
September, 2008

* I want to offer my heartfelt thanks to Diane Anctzak and Michelle Landau for their thoughtful and meaningful editorial help with these indroductory comments.

Author's Foreword

WHILE THE OVERWHELMING RESPONSE TO THE MONOGRAPH OF **The Way of the Image** was very positive, and many readers were even excited to discover an objective way to approach unconscious material, some readers wrestled with two issues.

The first came from people who read the monograph from general theoretical interest. They seemed to come up against an epistemological issue: the orientational approach involves getting to the essence of things. Isn't deciding what is essential about something quite subjective, thus going to the very core of the orientational approach?

At first blush it might seem to be the case. Historically, however, great thinkers from Plato on have had no problem deciding what is essential. Jung, as an example, takes it for granted that symbols have a very specific meaning. In his works on alchemy, he pays due respect to personal, subjective associations, but then, when he turns his attention to dreams with alchemical motifs, he proceeds to elucidate them by ascribing an objective meaning to the symbols. A recent publication of Jung's seminar on **Children's Dreams** (2008), reads like a straightforward application of the orientational approach, although somewhat lacking a precision that the approach ideally can bring to bear to the material. It is possible for good people to agree upon the core of an image in a given context.

The second reaction, and a very strong one, came from clinicians, who read the manuscript as a practical guide to the application of the approach. They seemed to be overwhelmed by the amount of knowledge that the approach requires. There is no way of avoiding this difficulty. The orientational approach is hard. It requires an extensive given knowledge, or the willingness to acquire it, constantly doing research, and expanding one's knowledge. (See the essay on **Angels** in this book for an illustration of how a precise understanding of an image leads to a dramatic clinical solution to a difficult case.) After all, it is much easier to ask someone, "What do you feel about the image?" than to reflect and get to the bottom of what a symbol means.

It is no secret that depth psychology, or psychoanalysis, does not occupy the central role that it held until 20 years ago. If we are to have any hope of reclaiming for analysis the role it deserves, we have to put the discipline (I use the term advisedly) on a firm basis, that includes a clear methodology, ways of validation, and precision, getting away from the rather vague and impressionistic ways that have led to so much ambiguity and discontent in the past. I believe the orientational method places analysis on a firm, scientific, provable basis.

Yoram Kaufmann
August, 2008

Introduction

For more than 50 years, C.G. Jung investigated the contents of the collective psyche. Like the autonomic nervous system and the innate ordering processes found in the outer natural world, this repository of collective experiences and wisdom reflects humanity's relationship with a world existing beyond the bounds of traditional human consciousness. Like the mystics and poets who sought guidance from the heavens, and now the physicists who speak of an intelligent universe, Jung taught us to look to the Self for a greater understanding of the inner and outer world.

While this domain of knowledge remains eternally available and accessible, humanity has unfortunately continued its march into the realm of the known—seeking guidance from an ego-based perceptual field. Like the Sufi story, which tells us about a man who lost a valuable object inside his home but searches for it outside where the light is better, we too seek out convenient outposts from which to apprehend the movement of the Self. Perhaps even more unfortunate is the current trend in the post-modern Jungian movement, whereby archetypes and their symbols are shaped to the contours of human design and consciousness. Perhaps we have made an all too literal interpretation of God's injunction that the world be made in His own image and likeness. Truthfully, I find it hard to believe that this God meant for us to shape the world into *our own image*. But that is exactly what happens when we simply rely on our own frame of reference to understand these non-personally, transpersonally inherited images. Humanity has gone to great pains to keep abreast with nature, matching step-by-step, invention-by-invention to prove that when the dust settles, we alone will be left standing. Pugilists to the end in a battle that ultimately we can never and will never win. Neumann, in **The Origins and History of Consciousness** (1954), suggests that ultimately, nature will prevail despite humanity's greatest attempts at dominance.

Beginning with Freud's keen interest in those unknown factors that shape and disturb our personality, psychology's venue was the subterranean domain, the witches' brew, the Freudian unconscious that houses our dreams, fantasies, and hopes. While Freud's courage in venturing into the taboo and unspeakable aspects of human nature should be applauded always, he rested too early in his creation drama and in attributing the contents of the unconscious only to those repressed, forgotten, and dreaded elements of the individual psyche.

Jung's foray into the unconscious yielded door upon door and room upon room of previously unknown and unexperienced levels of the human psyche. He found that these inherited aspects of the psyche were related to, yet fundamentally different from, the contents of the Freudian unconscious. Instead, Jung found vestiges of an archaic, non-personally acquired unconscious that was the true shaper of human consciousness.

As Jung struggled against the backdrop of Freud's parochial model to the unconscious, and despite the threat of father-Freud's withdrawal of support, Jung's investigations into the "Objective Psyche" continued. An approach to human nature, which previously had been the privileged domain of theologians and mystics, was now accessible to Jung and the first generation of Jungians. Spirit, Psyche, God, innate knowledge, and the "Objective Psyche" became relatively synonymous to describe a personality that transcended personal experience.

The first and second generation of Jungians, including Marie Louise von Franz, Esther Harding, Barbara Hannah, Carl Meier, Aniela Jaffe, Mario Jacoby, and Adolf Guggenbuhl-Craig, all advanced a view of psyche that had more to do with innate human nature and innate ordering processes than about the prevailing psychology of the 1930s, which centered on learning theory and cognitive psychology.

Jung's approach quickly gained a solid footing in diverse settings, including medical psychology, therapy, theological circles, and in time, even in the physics of Wolfgang Pauli. In fact, Jung's psychology has seen a tremendous renaissance beginning in the 1980s with the discovery of the "new sciences" of chaos theory, non-linear dynamics, dynamical systems theory, and the sciences of emergence. Jung's findings about the objective nature of the psyche and the existence of an innate wisdom paired well with the evolving worldview espoused in the new sciences. Pioneers such as David Bohm, Ervin Laszlo, Mae Wan Ho, David Peat, and Beverly Rubik, among others, found a language for the mysterious and beautiful domain each had discovered in their respective fields. Jung's vision had found yet another arena within which to grow. Unfortunately, however, while his discoveries were flourishing in these new fields, his own disciples were all too quickly abandoning the ideas of the "Objective Psyche" and of the Self's tendency for self-organization. In their place, his central ideas about the autonomy of the psyche were being eclipsed by a more simplistic, personalistic approach. I call this newer Jungian perspective a "subjective relativistic approach" because of its emphasis on an individual's thoughts, perceptions, and feelings as the *Via Royale* to the psyche. This *Via Royale* to the unconscious may all too soon become the *Via Dolorosa*. It is hard to believe that something as profound as Jung's discovery of the archetypes could be viewed as the purview of ego perceptions.

Fortunately, there is a voice in the Jungian world, one among just a handful of individuals around the world who recognizes the inherent wisdom of the human psyche and the need to admit the limitations of human consciousness when approaching the archetypes.

Dr. Yoram Kaufmann, a Jungian analyst who originally trained as a physicist in his native Israel, later trained as a clinical psychologist and then a Jungian analyst at the C.G. Jung Institute of New York.

Perhaps his early training in physics and his native understanding of the reality of the psyche allowed him to push through the limitations of our cultural lure toward simplicity. He is a rigorous investigator, a demanding teacher and supervisor, and brilliant analyst, whose grasp of the workings of the Objective Psyche stands him as one of the true leaders in the field of Jungian psychology and, for that matter, of modern psychology. For more than 30 years, he has taught about the limitations of conscious awareness while extolling the virtues of the Objective Psyche.

When he works with images, he is relentless in his search for the dominant and essence of an image. Unlike many of us, he is not tempted to make an image fit his own belief system. If, for instance, one dreams of a shark or a giant squid found in a local river, he will quietly listen to our thoughts and associations to these images, but we can trust that he will also at some point remind us that sharks and squid rarely, if ever, are found in fresh water and likely may not be able to survive in that environment. So for Dr. Kaufmann, the nature of an image, not our rendering of it, is of the utmost importance.

Just take a few minutes and read the work of contemporary Jungians and you will see that we have lost touch with the objective nature of the archetypes. Instead, we find a proliferation of subjectively morphed distortions of images and symbols. Remember that Jung suggested that we *allow the image to reveal its own nature*, rather than impart a meaning onto the image. While images and archetypes may benefit from the assistance of human intervention, we only do them an injustice when we try to understand them in anything other than their own natural, native context.

Toward the end of his life, Jung felt that in order to advance our understanding of the psyche, we would have to begin an interdisciplinary study of the archetypes. In some exciting and unexplainable way, the Assisi Conferences are on this path, and now for the past 15 years, have advanced Jung's understanding of the "Objective Psyche." Our ongoing dialogues with physicists, biologists, philosophers, musicians, artists, and consultants attest to our longstanding interest in the autonomous psyche.

Standing behind our many years of work is Dr. Kaufmann, whose profound and never-ending fascination with the psyche remains the major influence in my own and our Assisi community's professional life. Since 1979, when I began training as a Jungian analyst, Dr. Kaufmann has been the guiding influence in my work. More than 20 years ago, when I was still recovering from the ravages of a parochial education, and more failing grades in math and science than I care to remember, he introduced me to Zukav's **Dancing Wu Li Masters**. Written as a modern day equivalent to *Quantum Physics for Dummies*, I read this book with rapt attention. For the first time I heard about the fascinating world of quantum mechanics, of fields, and of the beauty of nature as seen through the eyes of a scientist. Little did I know that Zukav and Beverly Rubik, a colleague and fellow Assisi faculty member, were sitting in pubs in California back in the 1970's collectively discovering the works that were to become the fundamental ideas in the new sciences.

Next, during my doctoral studies, I selected Dr. Kaufmann and Dr. Robert Langs as committee members. In doing so, I had two of the greatest minds of our time on my team, and the electricity in the room with them was palpable. As if on cue, and following some grand design that I wish I had been in on, Dr. Kaufmann must have sensed that since I had survived my earlier foray into quantum mechanics and the new sciences, I should prepare for the next transition. He dropped the term *catastrophe theory* into the conversation. I was again off and flying. While I had no idea what this term meant aside from its more obvious references to things being in total disorder, I sensed that this word and the world of inquiry lying behind it represented a vital part of my future. Somehow, I think there was something intentional and a little bit mercurial in his actions.

Did Dr. Kaufmann know that what he had offered me was more important and valuable than what any other individual had ever given me? Did he realize that these early contributions would seed a movement now consisting of more than 20,000 individuals worldwide, all part of the Assisi community?

The richly textured layers of his life are evidenced through the beautiful and meaningful life he and his lovely wife Rise have shared for so many years. I will never forget how he told me one day of his deep love for Rise. For much of his adult life which he has shared with Rise, he has included his beloved dogs, has swum with the dolphins, and has filled his warm and welcoming home with the beauty of orchids. His practice as a senior analyst is enriched by his knowledge of the body and of the merits of complementary medicine. He has served as a Faculty Member, Board Member, and supervisor at The C.G. Jung Institute in New York and for The C.G. Jung Foundation. During his many trips home to Israel, he generously offers lectures and seminars to the local Jungian groups. In all, this has been and continues to be a rich and illustrious career.

I have tremendous love and respect for Yoram Kaufmann. He has provided me with the opportunity for a wonderful personal and professional life. He is, in every sense of the word, my mentor, my friend, and my family. I only hope that the ideas in this book touch all the readers as much as they have already touched an entire generation. You will never be the same after reading this work, and I trust there will be some "catastrophically" wonderful changes in your life as a result.

With the deepest gratitude, respect, and love,

Michael Conforti
Brattleboro, Vermont
April, 2004

The Way of the Image

The Orientational Approach to the Psyche

A TREE FALLS IN THE FOREST. DOES IT MAKE A SOUND, EVEN IF THERE IS no one to hear it? In fact, does the tree fall at all unless there is someone to see it fall? Or, to put it another way, is there an objective reality, or is there only subjective experience? This issue, the nature of reality, has been the subject of passionate debate since people started to contemplate the nature of reality. The pendulum has been swinging between two poles: the belief in a reality that is essential and independent of an observer, and a view that phenomena do not exist on their own, but come into being through the instrumentality of the observer.

These two views can be called essentialism and constructivism. The latter is part of a trend called post-modernism, which challenges the existence of facts. In psychoanalytic circles it has led to movements like subjectivism, intersubjectivity, narrative, and so on. Let me state at the very beginning that I am, following Jung, very much an essentialist.

Recently, they discovered in France cave paintings that are supposed to have been made more than thirty thousand years ago. Are we to say that these paintings had not existed prior to our discovery of them? It is my position that these paintings have existed all along, whether we saw them or not. Post-modernism tries to enlist the aid of physics to bolster its position, and rely, for instance, on quantum mechanics, evoking, quite erroneously and out of context, Heisenberg's uncertainty principle, which, contrary to popular notions, does not say that things are uncertain—quite the contrary.

So, do we discover or invent, mathematics for example, or the laws of physics? While stating that I am an essentialist rather than a constructivist, I am, of course, not ignoring the importance that perception has on apperception. There is an extensive body of knowledge in general, and experimental psychology in particular, which documents the whole range of factors that influence what we perceive. There is no denying that to a very large extent we do construct our reality.

We are, for instance, very much influenced by our culture, our environment, our past and our upbringing, to name just a few of the forces that shape what we perceive. But does it really follow that there is no objective reality out there? Both students of journalism and trainees in police academies undergo the same experience: at one point in their training a complicated happening is staged in front of them. They are then asked to describe what they had witnessed. Inevitably, the descriptions vary widely. This is done to impress upon the participants how unreliable eyewitness testimony is. **But it does not imply that the events did not occur**. It just points out how difficult it is to ascertain what actually happened. It implies that with proper training it is possible to get to the point of seeing what is there, rather than imposing a subjective reading of a situation.

In fact, a large part of proper scientific training is devoted to that goal—separating what is really there from what we want to, or are afraid to, see. A part of the training that Buddhist priests receive consists of viewing staged events. The students are then asked to say what conclusions it is legitimate for them to infer from the facts, and what are not. Again, the student priests learn how easy it is to misperceive, but nowhere is the implication that there is no reality out there!

It is no wonder that there is such a backlash against the notion of a fixed, objective, non-relativized reality. It immediately raises the issue: Who is to determine what the reality is? It sets up certain people as the knowers, bringing up the specter of malignant power. A very long and unhappy world history has painfully taught us to be very cautious of authoritarianism. A great many abominations have been perpetrated during the last few thousand years by people who claimed to possess the truth. It makes us all allergic to a pretender to the truth. Since, in addition, the people who have dominated the world, both for good and evil, have been men, this has taken on a gender issue. Authoritarianism is seen, not without cause, as patriarchal and due to male dominance. The atrocities, like the inquisition and the holocaust, committed in the name of truth have left a profound distaste and suspicion of any claim to an unyielding truth. Objectivity has been severely tainted and subjectivity is exalted.

How do we reconcile this pair of opposites: objectivity and subjectivity? It is always psychologically dangerous to get caught in a duality. A duality is a good, and sometimes necessary, starting point, but ultimately it needs to be transcended. The solution to the above dichotomy is subjectivity within clearly defined guidelines: diversity among pre-determined options. To illustrate: Since I was five years old, it was my privilege to be taken by my parents to a subscription with the Philharmonic every few weeks. For close to 30 years, I listened to the best performers. Inevitably, I got to hear the same piece of music played by different artists: Beethoven's fourth piano concerto, for instance, by Artur Rubinstein, Myra Hess, Robert Casadesus, Claudio Arrau, etc. It is a mark of their artistry that each one of them imbued the music with their own individuality, which was very distinctive. I used to be able to tell, by listening to a record, who the performer was. However, *they all played the same score!* The objective reality was the written score, the notes in a particular key, in a specific sequence. The subjectivity was the particular shading, the individual nuances, the subtle variations in rhythms and loudness, the different emphases. Thus, it is possible for a musical critic (like George Bernard Shaw, for example) to write that a particular performer took considerable liberties with the music, but it was all well within the spirit of the composer, whereas another artist infused the music with so much of his individual personality that it was no longer the piece written by the composer: Subjectivity was no longer within the well-defined boundaries, it was no longer bowing to the dictates of the objective reality.

So, behind the subjective mist there lies an objective reality. This objective reality is a solid, firm structure. One recalls Michelangelo's famous saying that when he was carving a particular piece in a stone he was really only uncovering what was already there. Then there is the physiological parallel: all of the six billion people who presently inhabit the earth are completely different, yet share an amazingly elaborate common ground—anatomy, metabolic processes, etc.—an enormous subjectivity obeying very well-defined constraints. Religion, as well, has struggled with this issue for centuries: The debate was between the "absolute truths" proclaimed by the Catholic Church and the Protestant view that the Christian dogma needs to be relativized. Important philosophers like Immanuel Kant spent considerable effort to try and grapple with these issues, with mixed results.

What it comes down to is a pair of opposites: Taken to extremes, we get rigidity on one side versus total fluidity on the other. Morbidity and paralysis vs. Chaos and randomness. We get a hint that this is, in fact, a false dichotomy, when we discover that under a seeming appearance of chaos there is an underlying deep structure. The creative reconciliation of this tension is **an innate structure underlying variability.** Real creativity may be defined as a welding of the subjective with a given, **_pre-determined_** structure, which is comprised of a set of guidelines and mandates. In Jungian theory, **the mandates and guidelines arise from the image or symbol.** The image carries within itself an inherent set of constraints, whatever one's subjective reactions to it happen to be at the moment. When we relate to an image from a subjective point of view, we **_interpret_** the image; when we relate to its objective structure we are **_translating_** it. We translate from the imaginal language to a psychological one, as we could translate it into any other language: musical, religious, architectural, political, etc.

Jung himself was clearly, despite some recent attempts to depict him otherwise, an essentialist. This is the whole meaning of the concept of the collective unconscious; or, as Jung came to call it later in life, the Objective Psyche. That is the essential power of the image: It brings with it a set of mandates and guidelines. When we encounter an image we have to determine what **dominants** or **radicals** lie behind the image, and this, in turn, will determine what set of constraints are involved.

Thus, from the psyche's point of view, the image is the carrier, par excellence, of energy. Our psychic system is, energetically speaking, not a closed system, but, on the contrary, a system capable of spontaneously regenerating itself, via the emergence of images. To repeat, images are our generators of energy. Everything that has ever been created was preceded by an image—streets, a blender, theory of relativity. Thus, we have the power of images for immense good or horrible destruction. All the history of mankind is, in essence, the unfolding of a series of images. Religions, of course, are sets of images that exert a very powerful force on their adherents.

The ability to generate images and relate to them is a measure of mental health. One could construct a nosology of psychopathology based on the facility with which a person is able to let images bubble up from their unconscious. In true depression, for instance, there is marked constriction of the ability to produce images. Obsession, or addiction, can be seen as a fixation on one image (or one set of images), as the bulimic or anorexic is fixated on the image of the thin body, or the fetishist is fixated on the high-heeled shoe. Boredom, which is an attenuated form of depression, is also a temporary suspension of the spontaneity of images. This ability is so vital to us that its blockage can lead to suicide. Images, of course, are ubiquitous—in literature, poetry, drama, music, opera, myths, fairy-tales, fantasies, day-dreams, and, of course, in dreams.

In classical psychoanalysis, images are interpreted, not translated. When an image appears, the person is asked to associate to it: "When you see an apple, what comes to your mind?" As Jung's association experiments have amply demonstrated, once you start associating to an image you will, sooner or later, depending on the valence of the image for you, hit a complex. In fact, Karen Horney, in her book **Self-Analysis**, recommends free-association as a method for examining one's unconscious. The prescription is very simple: start anywhere, and soon you'll hit a complex; continue as much as you can. After you've done that for a while, you'll be able to look back and see where you've hit your complexes. Thus you get a map of your complexes. This process does not depend on your starting point. Where does the specific image come in? How does the image get its power? What about a dream, which has many images in it? If all we do is associate to the images, then what is the purpose of receiving these specific ones? The answer is that these very specific images bring with them an energy that contains a *transformative* potential. The transformative energy is expressed by these very images, and no others. Although the message contained in the images may be expressed sometimes in simple words, these words, while correct on a cognitive level, will simply not have the same impact on the psyche as the emotional wallop as the images. This is why self-help books rarely help (which is why there are so many of them); what they say is usually quite true, but because they do not express their message in an imaginal form that resonates with the specific individual at a given time, they usually fail to impart a lasting, transformative effect. It's all very well to tell someone that they need to learn to trust themselves; but if this is expressed with the help of images that contain the requisite transformative power, the message will come through loud and clear. Now this may sound strange coming from a Jungian analyst who believes in a collective unconscious and the universality of archetypes, but the astonishing fact is that every individual has within themselves a unique set of images peculiarly their own. They speak ultimately to them. Although such images may be shared with others, and those others may be affected, they will not be affected equally, and they will not share in the transformative energy to the same degree. ***It is both the science and art of analysis to find this unique imaginal language for every analysand.*** Although from some point of view we end up saying the same to all analysands ("To thine own self be true," etc.), we only succeed to the degree that we find a resonance with the particular imaginal world of the particular individual.

Here we have a wonderful example of the complex interaction between the individual and the collective: While the underlying issues may be common to all mankind, they express themselves very differently and specifically in every individual. This is not dissimilar to the way the very same components of DNA combine in each person to produce a slight variation on a common theme: while we are all basically the same, and would appear so to someone from Mars, we are also quite unique. The same patterns obtain, but they manifest themselves quite differently. As Sheldrake might have remarked, every acorn has the blueprint for a mature oak tree; but all oak trees, although similar enough to one another to form a distinct biological category, are also sufficiently different from one another.

If we associate to an image we will finally hit a complex, but this complex does not necessarily contain the required transformative energy. In fact, more often than not, the associative process will only serve to allow the person to run away from the reality of the image, and to flee from what needs to be looked at. In classical psychoanalytic terms, it serves the purpose of the resistance; in Jungian terms, it serves the shadow side of the determination to get at the truth, for although people come in to analysis because part of them wants, or needs, to know more about themselves, this is not the whole story—there is also a side, sometimes a very powerful one, which would rather not know and which feels quite comfortable with the way things are. It is this side that would produce associations that will lead away from the perhaps unpleasant aspects that the image is trying to focus on. A case in point is an analysand who came to see me after an essentially unprofitable long analysis with a colleague. Among other things, her dreams involved in a recurring way the figure of her cleaning lady. The dreamer had very positive associations to this lady, and she and her analyst concluded that the cleaning lady represented a positive mother figure, compensating for a rather unfortunate mothering experience. This, however, led nowhere, and when I asked the dreamer to tell me about her real relationship with her cleaning lady, it very soon emerged that the cleaning lady was, in effect, a very angry, bitter, sadistic, sarcastic and self-involved person, who felt she had missed out on life, not using her considerable potential but settling on a marginal mode of living. So, clearly, that was the shadow side that was trying to make itself known to the dreamer; being in the shadow meant that she did not have sufficient access to it consciously, and was unconsciously identified with it, being lived out by her unconsciously. Understandably, the dreamer was not eager to face up to that aspect of her personality (who would?), and her psyche found a way to circumvent that necessity by bringing up all these wonderfully positive associations. Let me stress that it is not a matter of intelligence; the dreamer is an exceedingly bright woman, but no matter what our intelligence, when it really matters, our capacity for self-deception is truly monumental. So the unwary analyst was led down the garden path, both basking in a very "positive," so-called "supportive" atmosphere, which was, of course, quite detrimental to the dreamer, as her very real issues were not being addressed. As a not unimportant aside, it has to be said that there were also dreams that were telling the analyst that he was botching up the analysis, but he was equally unable to read those dreams correctly.

How are we, then, to approach the understanding of an image? How are we to avoid being led astray by associations whose very goal is to direct us in the wrong direction? We have to try and look at the image ***objectively***. We have to study the very nature of the image, what is essential about it; what makes it what it is and no other; what are its roots and what dominates it— its radicals and dominants. This is sometimes relatively easy, and at other times, quite complicated. It can lead to fierce arguments as to what is really essential about a given image (or situation, or person), but this very real difficulty should not discourage us from making the attempt to establish the objective reality of an image. It is like defining the image by virtue of a system of coordinates and the place of that image in this system of coordinates. This system of coordinates I call the ***orient*** of the image, because it orients us as to the nature of the image. At its simplest from, the orient is simply the context.

For instance, let us take as an example the not uncommon image of being naked. The objective dominant behind nakedness is vulnerability, but there are, of course, all kind of vulnerabilities. Being naked in a locker room, where being naked is appropriate, implies a very different kind of vulnerability from being naked in the street, which might realistically lead to one's arrest. The context of the locker room is different from the context of the public street; being naked is appropriate in one circumstance and inappropriate in the other.

Here we can also learn how personal associations interact with the objective nature of the image. One might protest that someone may not feel vulnerable at all about their nakedness, in fact, might enjoy it; that only tells us what their relationship to their vulnerability is. If someone who is very comfortable with their nakedness has the image of being naked in the street, it follows that the particular complex the image is trying to bring to consciousness is that they are very comfortable about being inappropriate. The inappropriateness might translate into tactlessness; and whereas many people feel (properly) embarrassed at their lack of tact, this person clearly does not. That is their complex, and they need to be made aware of it and its consequent ramifications from an interpersonal point of view: how they come across, and why they get the reactions they do. Some orients are very simple; most are complex, and require long, detailed study. This places quite an onus on an analyst who wishes to use the orientational approach. It requires little expertise to ask someone what they associate to an image, whereas it may take some thorough study to establish its orient. More importantly, it requires the analyst to take a stand, to become "opinionated," so to speak, and this may arouse in them their "power" complex, as it is so often called. Analysts who are not comfortable with that aspect of their personality very often prefer to maintain a non-committal attitude, preferring everything to come from the patient, as it were, rather than being the pronouncers of truth. Admittedly, pretending to know the truth can lead to gross abuse, and having a claim to objectivity can only be done with the utmost humility, always allowing for the archetypal nature of doubt: having a sense of rightness about something (an orient of an image, for instance) should not preclude the possibility of error. A wise person knows that knowing inherently also involves not-knowing, but this does not lead to the denial of the knowing: real wisdom consists in holding the knowing and the not-knowing in creative tension. Lack of the wisdom can be productive of arrogance and pomposity. *Caveat scientior!*

With this admonition in mind, let us turn to an example. But before we do that, we have to tackle an issue that arises naturally from the orientational approach. We are, in fact, positing that the inherent, objective qualities of the image are not only known to the analyst, but are available and pertinent to the person in whom the image arose. Let us reflect on that for a moment. Science is built around hypotheses, series of assumptions that lend themselves to verification or refutation. One can roughly divide hypotheses into two kinds: weak and strong. A weak assumption is one that does not strain our credulity too much, that is not too far from what we know or expect; a strong assumption, on the other hand, takes us into realms hitherto avoided or discarded.

Thus, Freud's hypothesis that adult behavior is reducible to the way one has negotiated one's passages through the awakening of one's sexuality is a weak hypothesis, since everyone is aware, at least to some extent, of their sexuality; and since sexuality is, to a lesser or greater degree, conflicted for everyone at one time or another in their lives, the fact that it might have something to do with the way we sometimes behave is not beyond the ken. Indeed, this assumption pre-dates Freud by at least several hundred years, and can, for example, be found in Shakespeare. This is one of the many reasons why Freud's ideas have served such a powerful myth: while on the one hand shocking, it also resonates with things we know about ourselves.

It is quite otherwise with Jung's hypothesis of the collective unconscious. This is a very strong hypothesis. It does, at least initially, strain our credulity, except for those of us who are, for want of a better term, more "mystically" inclined, and for whom this strong assumption seems natural and obvious. To state the hypothesis in its simplest form is to say that a rose is a rose is a rose, whether the person looking at a rose knows it cognitively or not. Thus, the provision for the knowledge about the rose is in all of us, inherent in our humanity. That is, indeed, a very strong hypothesis. But a hypothesis, strong or weak, is still a legitimate one if it can be submitted to the usual scientific methods of verification. Some of Albert Einstein's hypotheses in the special theory of relativity (like the constancy of the speed of light), and especially in the general theory of relativity (for instance, postulating that gravity, far from being a force the way we had been using to think of it, was, in effect a result of the curvature of space) are, after nearly a century, very hard to comprehend and very hard to swallow. Those are very strong hypotheses, but they have mostly stood the test of time, since most of the predictions produced by them have proven consonant with the data as we understand them today.

Let us now look at an example. Let us take the images of the shark and the octopus. Both are creatures of the deep, of the dark. We humans tend to attribute to things that we can't readily see all of the horrifying qualities that we are afraid of in ourselves; in other words, we tend to project on the deep and dark our own inner terrors. It is, therefore, not surprising that over the centuries people have tended to attribute both to the shark and the octopus frightening qualities. The projections on the octopus have, of course, been helped by the factual (i.e., objective) biology of the animal, namely its tentacles. So here are two images that inspire equal feelings of strong fear. It would not be surprising, then, that people would associate similar attributes to them, and evince comparable reactions to them. But viewed from an orientational point of view, they are quite different, because their objective nature is quite different. The shark is a very dangerous animal; although all is far from known about sharks, we do know that they are capable of "viciously" attacking humans, quite often maiming them severely, if not killing them. One had best stay clear of sharks, or if one has to deal with them, it best be done with some very strong protection. The octopus, on the other hand, is in reality a very gentle creature, which uses its tentacles mainly to sift through the salty water of the ocean to extract plankton (although it will use its tentacles as a wrestling arm if attacked by another of its species). A person swimming in the ocean need have no fear when encountering an octopus, and one may gently caress it. Here is how the orientational approach makes a difference: We have two distinct images upon which similar projections have been historically made. But the difference is this—in one case the projections correspond to the actual nature of the being, in the other the projections are quite contrary to the nature of the beast. What are the clinical implications of this difference? They are quite profound. Let us assume that a person has a dream in which a shark appears. This immediately informs the analyst hearing this dream that the dream is bringing up a real dangerous content of the unconscious; it is highlighting an unconscious complex that constitutes a real threat to the well being of the dreamer. That is the objective statement; that is the situation whether we like it or not. It is similar to results obtained in the course of laboratory blood and urine tests; they cannot be denied, but have to be dealt with. This factual statement from the unconscious has a compensatory quality to it. What it compensates depends upon the conscious attitude of the analyst and analysand. It may be compensating for the blindness of the dreamer as to the nature of his or her situation or psychology. Or, if the hearer of this dreamer is herself/himself unaware of this aspect of the dreamer, the image may be compensating for the blindness of the analyst in this regard, and may be calling for a re-evaluation of the clinical situation (more on that later). Neither the analyst nor the dreamer can be spared from the objectivity of the message, whatever their previous attitude had been. Now, where do the person's own reactions, (i.e., their associations) come into play? Do we dismiss them as irrelevant? Not at all. Of course, we do no such thing. The correspondence between the person's reactions and the objective reality of the image provides us with a very important measure of the degree to which the person is aware of their situation. The clinical situation becomes much more ominous if the person has pleasant associations to the shark; it throws into relief their need to deny the seriousness of their predicament. It is not surprising that sharks make their appearance quite regularly in the dreams of drug addicts. For instance, an initial dream of an analysand had him sitting on a rickety raft in the ocean, surrounded by sharks that were circling the raft. He turned out to be a serious cocaine user, and, not surprisingly, quit therapy shortly afterwards. The ego (in the Jungian sense, that is, the center of consciousness) was not up to dealing with this precarious situation, it lacked the appropriate tools, as was implied by the rickety raft.

Now let us take a second person who dreams about an encounter with an octopus. The image has a menacing feel to her while she is sleeping, and she wakes up in dread. Her associations to the octopus are the typical ones of danger and fear. Here the image is informing the dreamer that an aspect of herself that she had hitherto regarded as very frightening is, in effect, quite benign if she could only get close to it and learn to experience it first hand. As before, the image might come in this specific form to react to the analyst's misreading of the clinical situation, if, for instance, he or she had overestimated the degree of severity of a given psychic constellation. The unconscious then sends an image that means to amend the analyst's perspective, and it does so by sending an image to which the dreamer's associations are at variance with the objective reality of the image. ***In general, the degree of discrepancy between the objective reality of the image and the association to it indicate the extent of the complex.*** People who have no complexes in the area will give associations that are germane and relevant to the reality of the image. Precisely as in classical psychoanalysis, people who have worked through all of their neuroses should be able to truly "free-associate," people who have defused their complexes will be able to react to images in an appropriate, straightforward way.

But what if the person who gets those images does not know about the objective reality of those images? In our example, what if the person had no idea about the biological facts about sharks and octopi? The strong assumption that Jung has made in his concept of the collective unconscious is that it does not matter; that the *ego* may not know, but the *psyche* knows. It is a difficult hypothesis for many people to countenance, but it is a legitimate one. Now, a question that might intimidate even more the analyst who would like to use this method of translation: What if the analyst themselves does not know? This method presupposes a great deal of knowledge, but if the analyst does not know, they have to have a way of finding out. It is for this reason that one of the chief resources of a Jungian analyst is a good reference library, so that when the analyst encounters an image they are not well versed in, they turn to their resources to study the image.

It is more complicated when it comes to people who emerge as images in a person's material. Here one does not have a reference library, so that the analyst has to find a way to establish what the orient of a specific person is; that is, what is essential about that person in a given context, what makes them what they are, what constitutes their uniqueness. This applies equally to any piece of material that may emerge as significant for a particular person: the phenomenon of the Beatles, a movie, play, book. All this requires a lot of study and contemplation. Those are all the considerable difficulties involved in an orientational approach. On the other hand, properly and meticulously used, it can be seen that this approach considerably lightens the countertransferential burden from the oppressed analyst. We all, inevitably, have our biases, our prejudices, our pet theories. It is as it should be; that is the human condition. With the orientational approach we have a way of checking our impressions and reactions against the data. Much has been made recently of the use of one's own personal reactions as indicators about the nature of the therapeutic process, particularly by the British psychoanalytic school. Except in the hands of exceptionally gifted individuals, who have been thoroughly analyzed and have a highly developed ethical capacity, I'm not sure that this is a good idea.

To deduce from the fact that I'm feeling tired that something is going on with the patient (for instance, that they are not really present) seems to me a very dubious proposition. If I feel tired, it is most probably because I haven't slept well. I should be able to come to the conclusion that the patient isn't entirely there by observing them.

My reactions to patients are those of interest and curiosity, of attentiveness. If I have unusual reactions, I check them out against what I evaluate. This can be done equally well when trying to understand the meaning of an image. I can have hopes, fears, ambitions for the patient; but I have to be sure to validate those against what comes up, and be ready at any time to relinquish my most cherished beliefs. I believe that is what Jung meant when he admonished all analysts to learn and study as much as possible, and then at the beginning of every analytic hour to put that knowledge in a drawer.

Let us take an example. This is a dream presented by a Jungian analyst at a national conference. The dream is one of that analyst's patients. In the dream the patient and the analyst are scuba-diving in the ocean to a depth of three thousand feet. The analyst brought the dream as a demonstration of analytic work that achieves great depths. Obviously, both the dreamer and his analyst were impressed by the depth of the dive, and both took it as a very positive statement from the unconscious, giving them a good report card on the work that they had been doing. Looking at this dream orientationally, one would have to ask oneself what the orient of a scuba-dive is, and what the orient of the ocean in this context is. Whatever the personal association (of either dreamer or analyst) to three thousand feet is, one would be struck by the very specificity of the depth, and wonder about its significance. One may like and enjoy depth and associate good things to it, or one may be afraid of it; but whatever one's personal reaction it, we have to pay strict attention to the objective measure of depth supplied in the image. Here the orient of the ocean comes into play. If one did not know, one would have to study it.

One would find out, of course, that it is literally impossible to dive down three thousand feet. The pressure of the water increases drastically as one goes deeper, and after a while, long before three thousand feet, one would explode as a result of this pressure. So, the message that this image gives us is an unequivocal statement that the analytic process with this analysand is taking him to depths that perhaps answer the ambitions of the analyst, but are disastrous from the viewpoint of the analysand. He is being taken to depths that will tear him apart. Now, the knowledge about the pressure at the depth of the ocean is not arcane information; in this case, probably both participants were aware of this fact, but the point is, it does not matter. Even if the analysand does not know it, the analyst can supply this knowledge, **and this knowledge becomes part of the image.**

This is a radically different approach from the traditional one used to approach images. The word "dream" comes from an Anglo-Saxon root "treug" which means to deceive. It is characteristic of the long held view that dreams are there to hide the truth from us, no doubt because we have a tendency to project mistrust on things we do not readily understand. The Freudian view, as is well known, is that dream images are the permissible expression of inadmissible ideas: The dreamer "defends" herself/himself against unacceptable emotions or thoughts by going through an elaborate process of subjecting the original forbidden thought to distortions that produce the end result, a relatively benign representation of a taboo.

In classical thought, therefore, the goal of the image is to **hide**. As we have seen, our approach, which follows the Jungian approach, is that the image **reveals**. It contains within itself more than is evident at first blush. It is like an iceberg, where only the tip shows, but if you have the right attitude and the right tools you can discern a whole vast territory underneath it. As with a real iceberg, whether it becomes a danger or not depends on one's knowledge. In our example, the real important aspect of the innocent looking dive is inherent, latent, implicit, not on the surface. The surface may look benign, even enticing, as it obviously is to the analyst and his analysand. That is the trickstery nature of the unconscious, which, in our case, has seduced both participants.

But we haven't yet exhausted the richness of the image. We have dealt with the ocean and the depth. The other element that appears here is also very important: the scuba aspect. How do we deal with it orientationally? The first thing that strikes one when looking at the image is that while the ocean is a natural phenomenon, the scuba gear is man-made, and in that sense, contrived. It is telling us that this dangerous process of diving into the depths, in this particular case, disastrously, is not a process that is taking its own natural course, but, to the contrary, is one that is impossible via natural means, and is only possible because the dive is assisted by means of a contrived apparatus. Although I don't know (and we weren't told by the presenter) what actually took place in the analysis, I would venture to suggest that the analyst was using additional techniques, like guided imagery or active imagination, to so-to speak "deepen" the process, without making a proper evaluation whether the particular psyche of this analysand has what it takes to embark on such a perilous journey.

We get here a glimmer of a very important issue: Within the orient of the images lie explicit guidelines as to the **technique** to be used in the analytical process with a particular analysand at a given phase in the analysis. It is hard to overemphasize the significance of that statement. It is well known that all his life Freud avoided actually explicating what one really does in an analysis, despite his few papers on technique. The reasons were probably complex, not the least of which was that he did not want to give fodder to his detractors.

Jung did not leave us explicit techniques for very different reasons: being a great believer in individuality and in the "personal equation," he thought that different people would go after the same material in different ways, all getting, he hoped, to essentially the same results. This, of course, is quite naïve. People are apt to confuse the "personal equation" with a license to make therapeutic interventions in a haphazard and undisciplined way, without sufficient consideration to the appropriateness of the intervention. Since none of us is so completely analyzed so that complexes don't have their way with us, we should have some disciplined guidelines to steer us in the direction of the most fruitful intervention, and away from reactions that are going to be, at best, useless, and at their worst, misleading and dangerous. In our example, the major purpose of the image is to alert the analyst in general, that the analysis is heading in a dangerous direction, and, in particular, that the "man-made" adjuvant techniques that he is using are apt to cause serious damage to the analysand's psyche. If, as I surmise, these techniques involve some form of guided imagery, or, more ominously, active imagination, I believe the analyst is "ordered" by the analysand's psyche to cease and desist; re-evaluate the strength of his analysand's ego and readjust his technique accordingly. These claims that I'm making bring up various issues. Firstly, I am saying that the images that an analysand brings to the analysis, in whatever form, be it dreams, his behavior, body language, etc., contain, in addition to whatever psychic messages that they bring, also a set of instructions to the analyst as to what is the best, and sometimes the only, way to conduct the analysis. Contrary to what may have emerged at the dawn of the psychoanalytic movement, **there is no single technique that would be suitable for every analysand.** It has been a source of continuous astonishment and awe for me that in more than 30 years of practice, I have found that I work with every analysand in different ways.

To be sure, I have my style; nevertheless, the approach is unique to every individual and every situation. Furthermore, the style may change during the course of an analysis, as the needs of the analysand change. Several years ago I happened to be starting analysis with two people at exactly the same time. With one I adopted a nearly "classical" stance, saying very little, allowing for long periods of silence. This analysand was wrestling with demons in a way that would have experienced my interventions as intrusive and destructive. With the other analysand I talked a great deal, adopting more of a teaching modality, explaining to him how his psyche and other peoples' psyches function. The difference between those two ways of working was striking. I would like to think that the difference was due to their distinct needs, rather than due to an idiosyncrasy of mine, and I believe I could demonstrate it convincingly. I do not pretend to be saying that this way of reading the images in a manner that would instruct us about the specificity of the techniques to use is easily done. The guidelines are subtle and indirect. The method requires a capacity to extend what is being said beyond its immediate significance, to place elements of the picture in a wider context, although, sometimes, as in the diving example, the instructions are written in bold letters for anyone who is willing to see.

The second issue involved in this way of understanding images is a more fundamental one. We are, in fact, attributing to the psyche of the analysand a quality of being able to perceive the clinical situation with impartiality, of being able to process what it perceives and suggest remedies to rectify an incorrect approach if needed. That is a staggering hypothesis; again, as we said before, we would call it a strong hypothesis. Again, however, it is a legitimate hypothesis, amenable to verification or refutation.

Attributing wisdom to the psyche is a radical departure from classical analysis, and constitutes, in my opinion, one of the most fundamental (if not the most fundamental) differences between the Jungian approach and others. It brings in, inevitably, the spiritual issue. Are we nothing but the sum total of our repressed memories, or do we assume that we have, as humans, an inherent impulse, a spiritual reflex, that propels us toward a more evolved state of harmonious balance? The notion of a prospective gradient in nature in general, and in humans in particular, raises for some people an instant red flag. There is no avoiding the fact, however, that some phenomena do invite such an explanation, and one phenomenon that does that is the ability of the psyche to diagnose, evaluate and, in some measure, suggest ways of righting the situation. The positing of a teleological thrust seems to account for the facts in the most parsimonious fashion.

Let us look at a somewhat picaresque example of the way images bring with them a prescription for behavior. This did not occur in an analysis, but at a professional meeting of analysts, where one analyst, not known for sharing his inner world with colleagues, was talking about a recent personal crisis. He saw the crisis as resolved, and in support for this point of view brought in a lengthy dream as proof that he had overcome his difficult time. An important part of the dream involved a scene that took place in a swamp. The dreamer was standing in the swamp when he was bitten in his leg by a water snake. The dreamer experienced this as the "healing bite" by the Aesculapian snake. The analyst, who was clearly feeling very tentative about his understanding of the dream, and well aware that the images could invite a very different reading, said that he had felt reluctant to share this dream with us, as he was afraid that some of us would be tempted to offer our own interpretation. While he said that he looked straight at me, as if the danger of a contradictory opinion came primarily from me. He was quite right; I did have a much less benign view of his dream, but where he was utterly wrong was in anticipating my stating that view then and there. So, I said to him that if he truly understood the way I reverence the language of the psyche, he would know that since the bite was administered under the water, sub rosa, as it were, there was no way I would comment on his dream in the professional assembly, and he could rest assured and rely upon my reticence. To underscore the methodology applied here, let me reiterate: The major drama of the dream centers around the "healing" bite. The dreamer is being administered a dose of something. Whether the bite is truly healing as the dreamer believed it to be or not, that is not the issue. The most salient aspect of the drama is that it is done *in camera*, in private, under the water, out of anybody's sight (including the dreamer's sight, who only experiences the sting). So, the orient is that of privacy. It would therefore follow inevitably that whatever "healing" words one would want to say to this dreamer, it would not be obeying the orient of the dream to be telling him anything in a public forum. To put it in other words: The image brings with it an orient, and that orient imposes its rules and constraints upon the way in which one may relate to the image. Not to submit to these mandates is a violation of the spirit of the image, and may cause irreparable damage to the transformative capacity of the image; its energy may then turn somewhere else, sometimes in a very negative way. That is, perhaps, what a "sin" means in psychological terms.

A sin is a psychological mistake in which the orient of an image or a life situation is not meticulously obeyed. It is my contention, and we can only touch here very lightly upon this subject, that countertransference is precisely that phenomenon when the orient of a particular juncture in the analytic process is not sufficiently respected, obeyed, and submitted to. I know that what I am saying flies in the face of contemporary thought, which takes it for granted that countertransference is not only an inevitable, but, in fact, a very useful and desirable reality. Some therapists claim to rely on this reality as the main tool of their work. What I am saying is radically different: If one were able to adopt a precise, meticulous, orientational approach to the images as they present themselves in their myriad ways in analysis, there would be precious little countertransference. But that subject would take us far afield.

Let us, instead, turn to another example, which graphically demonstrates the distinct way an orientational approach brings to a set of images. This example is also special because it is not taken from an analysis. It was published in a book written by an analyst, and it is the writer's own dream, dreamt while he was contemplating on the various issues he was addressing himself to.

"In the dream I had been given a wonderful new opportunity to work in a musical setting in a job that had been vacated by a conductor known for his great musical gifts but also for his manipulative handling of personal relations. A much quieter, more introverted friend of mine, also a composer and a man of great personal integrity, had long been working in this space, and at first I felt that this was his world. But now I was to work here too, as the musical director. It seemed inconceivable that I, who can barely read music, would be able to function effectively in a leading position, but the other musicians were friendly, and I realized that from now on conducting them would be my job. In the dream it made sense that with daily practice I would soon get used to the musical notation and grow fluent."

Let us contrast the straightforward, take them as they come, approach to these images, with a strict orientational translation. If we take the images at face value, along with the emotions aroused by the context, we have a benign, reassuring message from the unconscious: It seems to be saying to the dreamer: "you have a much greater potential than you have realized. But fate has bequeathed you a much greater role; and, instead of encountering jealousy and animosity from your surroundings, you will encounter nothing but friendliness and cooperation from all around you. All you need is steady perseverance, and you will be rewarded." Who wouldn't want to hear that? We all like to think that we could function at a much higher level, and would like to believe that it always lies within our power to achieve it, especially without too much trouble. It is no wonder the dreamer feels very good upon waking up. But we have to look behind the obvious. Is the message what it seems like, or does it reveal hidden caverns?

The general orient here is that of music, and in order to understand the import of the images properly, one has to have some knowledge of music. The first important piece of knowledge that is required is that, contrary to what we may have been fed by old-time Hollywood movies, where people seem to be able to sing, dance, and play various musical instruments spontaneously, at the drop of the hat, without any preparation or rehearsals, in the real world musical virtuosity is acquired through hard labor: The reason Fred Astaire is able to glide spontaneously through complicated dance routines, either by himself or with a partner, is that he spent most of his life, as he himself was constantly pointing out, rehearsing and practicing. A consequence of that is that in music you have to start very early. It is totally impossible to start a serious musical career in your fifties. To be sure, if your dream has always been to be able to play the piano, and for whatever life circumstances you had been unable to devote time to study the piano, there is nothing that prevents you from taking up the instrument. You may, in fact, become reasonably good at it, able to play for yourself, and may be even good enough to entertain your friends. But we can be absolutely sure of one thing: You will never make it to the big league. You will not become a concert pianist. Now, this may seem harsh. We don't like hearing that something is closed off to us. Especially in the United States, the land of boundless opportunities, we would like to believe that if we but turn our mind to a goal, it becomes possible.

The Greeks, on the other hand, would have never been so naïve. They knew that the essence of being human is living with limitations, which only the gods, and sometimes not even they, could overcome. We have to bow to certain inevitability. In Cambridge, England, they throw "over-the-hill" parties to physicists who have reached the age of 30, because it is universally accepted that physicists do their most original and creative work before they reach 30. After that they can write, teach, turn to administration, but the godly spark will not touch them again. Even Einstein, in most respects the most unusual of scientists, did all of his groundbreaking work prior to the age of thirty, and although he directed a good amount of his prodigious talent to formulating a Unified Theory, he did not succeed, and turned his energies to fighting for peace and against the atomic and nuclear bombs. Music, a close sister to mathematics, imposes its own harsh constraints on those who wish to worship her, and for all of one's fervent desires, one cannot contravene those constraints.

That is particularly true about conductors. To the uninitiated it may seem that the role of the conductor is a very simple one. In fact, people have been known to opine that conductors are superfluous. What do they do, after all, except wave their baton to the rhythm of the music? The true musician, however, is well aware of the complexity of the conducting. According to Loren Maazel, an eminent conductor, the minimum requirement for a conductor is a perfect pitch. Now, perfect pitch is something that you are either born with or not; it is not something you can acquire. One may train one's ears to notes and intervals, but if one was not born with it, one will never have it. Some people might argue with Maazel about the absolute necessity of perfect pitch, but what is eminently true is that in order to conduct one had better know to play well at least one instrument, and preferably several; one better have an excellent ear, excellent musical memory, even if one conducts from a score. In short, one had better be a dazzling musician. What all this is leading to is the unavoidable fact that for someone who at mid-life is barely able to read music, it is utterly impossible, ***within his lifetime***, to become even a low level conductor, let alone take the place of an eminent conductor. It is also well known that professional musicians have little tolerance for incompetence and amateurism on the part of a colleague, and will not automatically accept a new conductor, but subject them to a rigorous period of evaluation. Their original attitude will be that of suspicion, requiring that the new kid on the block prove themselves. Orchestras have been known to refuse to play well with conductors they did not consider of a sufficient level. All in all, the scenario of the dream is filled with implausibilities, things that not only could not realistically happen, but are, in fact, the exact opposite of what would happen. It is pointing not to what could realistically happen, but, by reversal, emphatically stating that this utopian goal will not be achieved within this dreamer's lifetime.

Whatever the integration adumbrated by the dream is, the integration of a hitherto unaccessed part of the personality is not within the realm of the dreamer. That is the sobering, and perhaps harsh, message from the unconscious to the dreamer. "Accept your limitations! Make meaning of your fate!" So, we see that the orientational hermeneutics, via paradoxical reversal, conveys a directive that is quite in opposition to the one that the dreamer wished to believe. It does that by presenting two images that are diametrically different from their realities: the ability of a barely musically literate man to become a top-notch conductor, and the friendliness of the members of the orchestra toward a professional who is learning the ropes. This is a powerful dream, in the sense that it says something about the *fate* of the dreamer.

The idea that a dream is capable of making a statement about the fate of the dreamer is a far cry from the notion that a dream comments about the daily events, highlights a complex, or brings up a hitherto unconscious content for conscious review. It would not seem a strange idea to the ancients, who took it for granted that God spoke to us humans through images, and these divine communications inevitably took on a fateful dimension. We have come, in essence, a full circle.

We come to the end of our journey. We started with the concept that images are powerful carriers of energy; that they reveal, rather than hide, to those willing to pay attention. We postulated that images come not as strangers, but bring with them an inherent structure, sometimes obvious and clearly stated, at other times only subtly hinted at. We discussed the interweaving of our subjective reactions ("associations") to the images, and the objective, essentially observer-independent, dominants, and radicals that constitute the orient of the image. We established that true creativity comes from the mysterious conjunction of the original, unexpected, subjective, and the predetermined guidelines dictated by an orient, and saw that in Jungian psychology those guidelines are inherent and embedded in the image. Thus, the image can be translated on an infinite number of levels, where it obeys the same constraints at each level. Thus, the image can be used clinically for diagnosis and prognosis; for commenting on the analytic process, and, perhaps its most precious quality, it can specify the proper analytic technique to be used with a given analysand at a given time.

We hinted at the possibility that an orientational approach might considerably lessen the overpress of the countertransference, freeing the analyst burdened by a multitude of emotional reactions to listen in an attitude of curious interest. From subjective to objective, and objective to subjective: That is the way of the image.

April, 1996

The Way of the Image II

What Do I Say (or Don't Say)
An Orientational Approach to
Therapeutic Technique

A COLLEAGUE OF MINE WHO HAD TRAINED IN EUROPE TOLD ME HOW burdened the trainees were in the analytic institute where he was training by all the heavy theoretical subjects they were studying: analytic theory, myths, fairy tales, ancient texts, and so on. Then, out of the blue, an inspired instructor took pity on them and offered a course entitled "What do we say?" The students, apparently, heaved a gigantic sigh of relief. Up to that point nobody devoted any attention to the clinical issue of what, of all that heavy material, if any, was to be shared with the analysand, and, more importantly, in what form.

Freud, notoriously, wrote very little about technique. His professed rationale was that he did not want anyone distorting his methods, and these could not be learned from written materials, but had to be studied in an analytic institute sanctioned by him. Jung was no better in that respect. He assumed that he was writing to professional therapists who would know how to apply his theoretical insights in clinical practice. Moreover, Jung was, to some degree, formulating his ideas in contradistinction to Freud's "rigid" system, and was putting a very heavy emphasis on the "personal equation," that is, every person's uniquely subjective way of working. This has, unfortunately, led to a great deal of misunderstanding. More on that later, when we deal with the crucial issue of what kind of latitude analysts have in communicating with analysands.

Jung, for his part, also wrote very little about technique. He assumed (naively, as it turns out) that his readers were mostly experienced therapists and that he was writing about ideas and theories that complemented their knowledge. Marie-Louise von Franz (whom Jung apparently considered the one person who most understood what he was about) wrote extensively about understanding dreams and fairy-tales, but she never tells us what of her understanding, if any, would be communicated to the analysand. Thus, Jungian analysts are basically left on their own. In fact, one could be pardoned if one concluded that the first generation of Jungian analysts felt that it was enough for the *analyst* to understand the material; that, by itself, would lead to healing. I remember listening to a talk given by a senior analyst from Zürich. He was showing us an elaborate series of drawings an analysand had done during her work with him. He gave us an elaborate, intellectually stimulating, running commentary on the drawings. When he was asked what of his understanding of the drawings he shared with the analysand, it turned out that none of it was. He clearly felt that it was not necessary.

The issue of the range of techniques, while frequently on my mind, was brought to a focus for me when, synchronistically, I started to see two new analysands simultaneously. With one of them, I just listened for the whole session without saying a word (in fact, we both sat in silence for three-and-a-half years, after which he started to talk); with the other analysand, I talked quite a bit. This experience highlighted for me the issue of how we choose a particular way of interacting with a patient at a given time. Could we demonstrate a connection between the material presented by a patient and the requisite mode of communicating with them?

At one time I had a case seminar in my New Jersey office. It was a private case seminar, outside the aegis of an institute. The participants were therapists, some Jungian, some interested in Jung, and some therapists working in clinics in the New Jersey area. At our first meeting I was explaining what our approach was going to be. Among other things, I casually said, not realizing I was saying anything extraordinary, that we will try to tailor our techniques according to the material presented by the patient. One of the participants, who worked in a social agency, expressed her perplexity, as in her clinic all therapists were supposed to adopt the same technique to all patients, no matter their psychodynamics, pathology, or personality. Frankly, I could not believe my ears. When I asked what that general technique was, I was not surprised to hear that it consisted mainly in listening silently to the patient's narrative, making only rare and sporadic comments. The technique consisted mainly of silence.

In due course, I asked this therapist to present a case of one of her patients. The presentation included an initial dream, which the dreamer brought after a few sessions:

"I am in a foreign city. I don't know anyone. I am ill and I need some help. I try to ask directions to a hospital, but no one is willing to help me. I feel desperate."

Could there be a more touching cry for help? I think most analysts, of whatever orientation, unless rigidly wedded to a fixed technique, would promptly recognize that this dream is an obvious mandate from the psyche to change course, abandon the silent treatment and engage the patient in a creative dialogue, abandoning silence as being inappropriate to this particular patient at this time.

That is not an unusual situation. On the contrary, I maintain that this example is the rule rather than the exception: The Objective Psyche sends us guidelines and mandates, asking us to adopt a technique that would be the most suitable for a given patient at a given time. **Using an inappropriate technique by not following instructions coming from the unconscious will lead to a "wild analysis," a hit-or-miss process with unpredictable, not to say destructive, results.**

Let us now turn to another example. This time we are not dealing with a dream, but a spontaneous image that the patient brings up during therapy. Following a painful interchange with his therapist, he blurts out:

> *"I feel as if I am sitting on a round stage, surrounded by people I don't know, who are listening in on what I am saying. I do have some secrets."*

When this was presented to the members of my seminar, various possible responses to that image were offered:

Silence (not saying anything)

You have issues of trust

Don't you trust me?

You are afraid of my reaction

You have large issues with shame

Privacy is very important to you

Sharing is not easy for you

Why are you bringing this up now?

Are you angry with me?

Do you resent being in therapy?

Do you feel our relationship is "unequal"?

We have all kinds of responses: ones having to do with contents, the others with process ("transference") reactions. Is there a "right" response, or will they all do as well? It is comforting for therapists to believe the latter. After all, don't all roads lead to Rome? Well, actually they don't—some lead to Perugia, some to Pisa, and some to Napoli. I maintain that there is a right response, a correct one. What do I mean by "correct?" I will define a response being correct operationally when the response causes a change of energy, a palpable transformation occurs. I once had an analysand who had a severe flight phobia. After paying careful attention to his material for a while, I presented him with an image. The image made such a powerful impression that he was rid of his phobia, and is now flying regularly and happily without any problem.

The Way of the Image II

I am quite aware that the idea of a uniquely appropriate reaction will not find favor with most therapists. (When I was raising, at one of my lectures, the possibility that there may be a unique interpretation to an image or a dream, one of my colleagues attending flounced out of the room in disgust!)

Therapists cherish their individuality, the "personal equation." But before howls of indignation reach their peak, let us consider whether the idea of a single, unique response is, in fact, so egregiously preposterous. Most every one has had the following experience—you have a problem, something that you don't understand. You discuss the issue with various friends, all of whom give reasonable, plausible solutions and explanations. But you find them all unsatisfactory. Then someone puts the answer in such a way that you react, "Yes, that's it!" This particular answer might not substantially differ from all the other responses, but, somehow, in the way it was formulated, the emphases placed, it led to an instantaneous recognition of its rightness. In other words, it clicked with the person. We frequently have these experiences. An explanation that we had been looking for, and had hitherto eluded us, becomes crystal clear when it is put in a certain way. This could refer to the same contents expressed in a specific image, or to a different sort of explanation. What is important is that that explanation resonates with one, accompanied by a satisfying feeling of recognition of the truth of the observation.

In the same vein, I submit that there is an optimal "interpretation" of a given interaction or an image or a dream, one that brings about the most transformative energy. In the example above, the orient is the theater, where actors take on roles. The actor is the shaman, who uses secrets to ply his trade. Therefore, the most transformative response to the patient's interpolation is, "Yes, it is important to have secrets." This acknowledges the patient's right to have secrets and reassures him that he will not be forced to betray something until, and if, he is ready to. It is, above all, an empathic response. The supervisee who presented this patient reported that he was a very difficult patient; the therapy with him was going nowhere. After she started adopting the orientational approach, making precise responses to his comments, fantasies and dreams, she reported that she no longer was in the dark about the case that had opened up and the patient was making steady, although slow, progress. Her original reaction to the patient's last comment ("I do have some secrets"), by the way, was "Such as?"

The idea that there is a "correct" or "true" answer, raises, inevitably the thorny philosophical-epistemological question of the possibility of ever understanding the nature of truth and objectivity. The battle between the two sides—those that claim that objectivity exists and truth is attainable, and those that say that it does not exist—has been waged for more than two thousand years, starting with Aristotle to our modern age. Steven L. Goldman in his **Science Wars: What Scientists Know and How They Know It** lays out the lines of battle: a side claiming that there is a truth that is universal, necessary and certain, versus those who say that there is no absolute truth, only our experience to guide us. (Of course, where our experience failed us was in trying to explain planetary motion—our experience taught us that we are the center of the universe, and the stars and planets revolve around us. It took Isaac Newton's theoretical laws to give us a more accurate picture of our universe.)

On the side of certainty and truth is a formidable array of scientists-philosophers:

Plato, Aristotle, Descartes, Galileo, Newton, Hobbes, Locke, Kant, Laplace, Euclid, Fourier, Poincaré, Schlitz and Reichenbach, and Einstein.

On the side of the pragmatic view, of the primacy of experience over theory, is an equally formidable list of great scientists-thinkers: Sophists, Boyle, Berkeley, Hume, Herschel, Comte, Mach, Duhem, Hertz, Dewey, Bohr, Condillac, Fleck, and Kuhn.

Let us return to the issue of guidelines for technique derived from unconscious material with the orientational approach. Jungian analysts are exposed during their studies to an imaginal technique called active imagination. It superficially resembles a more well-known technique called guided fantasy, but it bears the same relationship to it as the classical technique of "free" association as applied to dreams has to the associative process in the Jungian dialogue. Classically, an association is anything that comes to the dreamer's mind—the association is by temporal contiguity. In the Jungian process, the association has to be relevant, otherwise the analyst may feel that the association, far from leading toward the issue raised by the dream, is, in fact, leading *away* from it, thus colluding with that part of the psyche that wishes to remain blind to it.

Active imagination is a very difficult, very powerful technique. It has a tremendous healing power if handled well, as well as a great potential for harm. Like a bad LSD trip it can over-stimulate the psyche, lead to over-identification with archetypal forces and lead to psychosis and institutionalization. It is, therefore, very important to know when it is prudent to use it and when it should be avoided. Of course, astute clinicians can form an informed impression without additional help, but we all sometimes can use guidance from the unconscious.

Here are some examples. A relatively inexperienced analyst is eager to try active imagination with an analysand. She brings in a dream that contains the following snippet:

"I am watering the plants in my apartment. They are not growing."

Clearly, pouring libido (energy) into this psyche is not going to lead to growth.

An example pointing in the opposite direction is the following snippet:

"I am planting lentil seeds into lentil holes."

Here the dream is saying that there is something very right about this dreamer: The dream ego (the dream's protagonist) plants the seeds in their appropriate place. Here, enriching the psyche can bear healthy fruit.

In general, we can glean from the patient's material as to how to proceed. We must base our therapeutic approach on our clinical understanding, and then be prepared to get course correction, so to speak, from our analysand's psyche.

The core of the orientational approach is **absolute faithfulness** to the material. This material can be a dream, a fantasy, a person's description of an experience, anything. I assume, a priori, that the patient's psyche says **exactly what it means.** That meaning is our only sure anchor, what keeps us from drifting way off course, pulled by the currents of our preconceived biases, our expectations for the patient, our own unresolved issues. The final arbiter of the meaning of the material is the material itself—not what it may stand for, not what it may be compensating for, but the material itself.

To be sure, understanding a particular image, or a particular turn of phrase, may be very hard to do. We may have to research the objective facts about that image. For example: Is the image of a parachute about finding a way to be safe in a potentially dangerous situation?; or about being exempt from the universal laws of the physical universe, such as gravitation?; or is it about transforming part of our nature (silk) through the intervention of the ego (manufacture) into something that can save our life? For another example: A patient says "I was hitherto unaware of that." Why the archaic word "hitherto?" Does it direct us to the time that "hitherto" was in general use? What does that particular time correspond to in the patient's life?

The orientational method is deceptively simple. A closer look, however, yields surprising depths. For instance, it can be applied in a geological manner to reveal an infinite amount of layers of understanding and meanings. One can look at an image (or a dream or fantasy) from any number of layers: psychic, psychological, religious, spiritual or soul layers. One can view it through an infinite number of orients: musical, botanical, sociological, historical and so on. One is only limited by one's imagination, and thus can gain unexpected insights into various fields and endeavors. Thus, the method can be extended both in **scope** and in **depth**.

The process involves two stages: first, the raw material—a newspaper headline, a proverb, a film, a book—has to be **translated** (not interpreted) into its exact psychological equivalent. Once this is accomplished, it can be directly applied to whatever orient we have chosen, provided, of course, that one possesses enough familiarity with the orient to be able to accomplish this. A possible benefit, thus, would lead to a more profound understanding of the orient at hand.

Let us take an innocent looking example. Here is a sentence that might appear anywhere in a fairy-tale:

The king summoned his vizier.

Our first task is to **translate** the expression from the orient of a fairy-tale into psychological language. What is the essence of a king? A king has many attributes, but the most fundamental is that he is a **ruler**. He rules over a territory.

Next, we come to the vizier. If one is unfamiliar with the term, it is time to reach for an appropriate reference book. (As a matter of fact, it is essential for someone using the orientational approach to have an extensive reference library.) There one would find that the term vizier refers to the king's main servant (or steward). So, now the fairy-tale phrase may be expressed as follows:

Whatever rules a territory summoned the force that is its main help in governing.

Now that we have expressed the fairy-tale idiom in psychological terms, we can apply it to any orient that we wish. For instance, we may use it as follows:

Divide your life, by age, into meaningful (to you) segments: for instance 0–4; 5–9; 10–16; 17–24; 25 onward. Then ask yourself for each temporal segment, what was ruling you during that time, and, once you have established that, what was most helpful to you to achieve that goal. For instance, during a certain segment you were ruled by your ambition to be an excellent student; you were helped by your considerable intellect. At another time, the most important thing to you (the ruler) was to be liked by the opposite sex, and your vizier toward that goal was your charm. Once you finished doing this for the important slices of your life, you will have a new lens through which to understand your life. You have a powerful tool for reflection, introspection, and meditation. And all this via one sentence! Not a special sentence, but any sentence.

The possibilities are endless. One can translate that sentence into any orient if one possesses enough familiarity with it. Take music, for example. There the ruler might be the tonic (chord) and the vizier is the dominant (chord). And so on.

Another possibility is to expand one's understanding to many levels. For instance, one could take a dream and look at it from a psychological level, a psychic one, religious, spiritual, or soul level.

All in all, the orientational approach allows one to navigate the length and breadth of the psyche.

The Analyst of My Dreams

SUMMARY: THE PHENOMENON OF THE APPEARANCE OF THE ANALYST in dreams of analysands has been a controversial issue, and is understood in a variety of ways by different schools of thought. An orientational approach to this phenomenon will be presented, and will be used to discuss the very crucial issue of boundaries in the analytic situation.

An analysand comes to his session and reports the following dream: "I am in my session with my analyst, except that my analyst is sitting in my chair, and I am sitting in his." What are we to make of this dream? What approach should we take to the understanding of this dream? The role that the appearance of one's analyst in an analysand's dream has been a controversial issue in psychoanalysis, and the field has had a variety of approaches to this thorny issue. In this section, we shall discuss several approaches to this phenomenon, and interlace this topic with the very crucial subject of boundaries in the psychoanalytic encounter.

Let us first attempt to place things in historical perspective. Psychoanalysis, as we know it today, was to all intents and purposes invented by Freud. From my point of view, there are essentially two very distinct aspects to Freud's legacy. The first aspect, where his genius came blazingly through and placed him along other geniuses like Charles Darwin and Albert Einstein in permanently altering the ways in which we think of ourselves, was in his resurrection of the unconscious to its prominent place. Freud, of course, did not invent the unconscious, as Henri Ellenberger's seminal work, **The Discovery of the Unconscious** makes clear. Freud was, however, to explicitly state that our behavior is not only motivated by factors of which we are aware, but, to the contrary, is largely based on causes of which we are either only dimly aware, or not at all. We are not really masters of our own house. Freud brought to light the fundamental fact that the unconscious communicates with us through symbolic means, usually via imaginal products; be it a daytime fantasy or nocturnal dream. Everything that the psyche produces is symbolic. This aspect of Freud's accomplishment is what will stay a permanent part of human consciousness forever.

The second aspect of Freud's legacy has to do with the consequences of that view of human nature. Now that we have postulated the symbolic nature of the human psyche, how do we understand it? In other words, when confronted with a fantasy or a dream, how do we interpret it, or, in a way that I prefer to think about it, how do we translate the images into psychological language. Here, Freud took a path that has been, to my mind, a very unfortunate one for psychoanalysis in particular and humanity in general. Whereas Darwin and Einstein proposed far-reaching and revolutionary theories, they still remained within the broad confines of Western science, the essence of which is that hypotheses are only useful if they allow us to generate predictions that are capable of being validated, and thus modified and altered as the need arises. In that sense, Freud did not give us a theory, but rather a dogma.

The interpretative method and developmental theory that Freud formulated are not capable of being verified or disproven. It has always amazed me how rarely, if at all, this very crucial fact is ever mentioned or discussed. The fact is that Freud's whole theory has as a major concept the idea of inhibition. Everything centers around this idea. The result is that a phenomenon can either be observed, or it is assumed to be, inhibited. In other words, one can never prove or disprove anything. From an axiomatic theory point of view, we have here a system in which any conclusion can be justified—whether the phenomenon is observed or, if it is not observed, is assumed to have been inhibited. A classical analyst is always right in his interpretation: Either the patient agrees, or s/he is resisting. Needless to say, good clinicians don't operate that way; they end up formulating for themselves criteria for the authenticity of an interpretation. The astounding fact remains, however, that Freud did not give us a set of hypotheses that can ultimately be proven, he gave us a dogma: a set of beliefs, which one either takes on faith, or doesn't—in other words, a religion, with all of its attendant rituals, blessings and intolerances. We have, in other words, a circular system, an infinite loop without an exit. The very essence of a scientific discipline is a provision for self-correction, through which one's beliefs can be challenged and modified. The consequences for classical psychoanalysis have been, in my opinion, disastrous: while the truly gifted analysts developed their own way of evaluating where and when an analysis wasn't proceeding smoothly, the majority of mediocre and bad analysts tried, come what may, to impose a belief system on their analysands, and when it did not produce the requisite results, the responsibility was assumed to be a result of resistance.

The first person who tried to break the circle was Wilhelm Reich, in his undervalued classic **Character Analysis**. Being a highly talented clinician, Reich had to face the fact that although he was making the "right" kind of interpretations (that is, he was following the theory as it was then currently espoused), insight did not always follow and neurotic patterns did not change. Being an essentially honest person, he was reluctant to ascribe all these misses to resistance. Maybe the problem lay with the method, not the patients. This led him to formulate his revolutionary theory of character armor, the consequences of which, from an interpretive point of view, were that it was not only the content of the interpretation that mattered, but its timing. So, the patients hadn't necessarily always been wrong, but were responding to faulty technique.

Historically, this was a revolutionary, bold step, but it was, in the grand scheme of things, only a very small step: Reich did not provide for a way for the system to correct itself, because he did not do away with the centrality of inhibition—the system was still infallible, it only needed a different methodology. Nevertheless, it was a very important step in that it recognized the reality that neurotic symptoms were stubbornly resisting the assault of "correct" interpretations, and that analysts had better look to what they were doing, rather than assume that the theory was right and the patients to blame for not improving despite the best efforts.

It took more than half a century for the next step to be taken. Robert Langs started publishing a series of books in which he took an essentially different approach—getting away from the dualistic view of analyst and analysand and the polarity of healer and wounded, healthy, and sick. For him the major variable is a field, a communicative field, that is constellated between them. In this field, the unconscious of the analysand is capable of detecting when and where the analyst is barking up the wrong tree, or is altogether wrong, where things are amiss. It is hard to overemphasize the importance of this new approach. Here we have a totally new paradigm. The ultimate wisdom is not with the all knowing analyst, but with the psyche, the unconscious of the analysand! This paradigm takes us totally out of the Freudian worldview—instead of the polarity of the two, we have a third, which, in Jungian terms, we might call the transcendent function; and to it is ascribed, appropriately, a wisdom which transcends the consciousness of the two participants. The hypothesis of a superior wisdom in the psyche is a totally foreign concept in the Freudian canon, where the unconscious is a reservoir of repressed, mostly primitive forces, to which realm they have been consigned by virtue of the threat that they pose to the conscious ego. More importantly, by virtue of his hypothesis, Langs is breaking the circularity of the Freudian system: This hypothesis permits making predictions, which can be validated or disproven. We are into science again, rather than a belief system! I believe it is this fact that has engendered the very hostile reaction to the Langsian paradigm, although the overt reactions are seemingly about something else (more about that later).

Strictly speaking, Langs' ideas do not apply to Jungian analysis. In his paradigm, Langs assumes the classical Freudian situation—the patient lies on the couch with the analyst at his back, and is instructed in the fundamental rule, which is to say anything that comes to his mind, via the so-called "free" associations (which are, of course, anything but free). The analyst keeps basically silent, allowing the associations to spin round and around. This is not the framework of a Jungian analysis, which should probably be more appropriately called a creative dialogue, since the analyst is actively engaged in an interactive exchange with the analysand. In Freudian analysis, the flow of the associations constitutes a kind of a "narrative," and it is the nature of the flow of the narrative that informs the Freudian analyst about the nature of the blocks the patient has to remember in order to overcome his various neurotic symptoms. It is also in these twists and turns in the narrative that the messages the patient's unconscious is sending out are hidden, and must be decoded by the analyst.

Why hidden? Here we come to a cornerstone of the classical Freudian Weltanschauung (sharing with Nietzsche the attitude of "suspiciousness" toward the world). The Freudian approach is founded on a basic mistrust of human nature: Things are not what they seem to be; what you see is definitely not what you get.

Although most of us lie sometimes, here the leap is to assume that everything we say, certainly about important matters, is naturally a lie. The conscious part of the personality, the ego, is constantly under a barrage of tumultuous, primitive impulses, largely unacceptable to the relatively civilized person. To avoid dealing with these impulses he has at his disposal a large repertory of ways, called defense mechanisms, that help the ego negotiate the treacherous onslaught from his unconscious. The role of the analyst is to unmask those subterfuges and reveal the hidden truths. The crucial consequence of this approach is that, in the Freudian scheme a symbol is there because it <u>hides</u>, whereas in the Jungian approach, a symbol is there because it <u>reveals</u>.

This leads us to the notorious issue of latent versus manifest content. Starting with the premise that we are constantly in the process of hiding from ourselves, it is natural to posit that the symbolic language we employ is primarily designed to hide. Indeed, in some of Freud's published case material the contents are clearly taken to represent the opposite of what it appears: for instance, let us take the case of the Wolf man (so called because a central dream of this man involves wolves). These wolves are standing still in the dream; Freud concludes, therefore, that they are moving! If this transformation from a manifestation to its opposite were applied consistently we could attempt to check its usefulness. But, as was mentioned before, this system of interpretation has at its disposal a whole armamentarium of transformations that can be applied without a predetermined rationale so that the interpreter of the image can arrive at any result desired. So, if you want to get at a so-called "sexual" understanding, all you have to do is employ the adequate transmogrifications of the various images and you get to where you wanted to be.

The Jungian, or orientational approach is quite different. Here, the image is taken to be a "just so" image. The image is not there to hide anything, but to reveal, bring to light, heretofore unrealized aspects. This is not to imply that the image is a sign, completely cognitively understood. The image is symbolic, in the sense that we know some aspects of it, but are ignorant, or only dimly aware of, other, deeper aspects of it. In the Freudian classical system you approach an image by "free" associating to it. This, inevitably, takes you, at least initially, away from the image. The classical analyst postulates that it is resistance that propels the associations away from the true nature of what the image is trying to hide, and assumes that by allowing the hapless patient to spin their associations for a long time the pressing energy behind the image will ultimately force, in a kind of centripetal way, the real issue behind the image to appear. Depending on the nature of the resistance, this can take years. As Jung makes graphically clear, his approach is radically different. In **Modern Man in Search of a Soul**, he illustrates his method by the saying that if a dreamer dreams of a "deal" table (deal is a kind of pine wood), then we are dealing (excuse the pun) with a deal table, not any other kind of table. Jung then looks for a relevant association to specifically a deal table: If the dreamer, because of their "resistance," then comes up with an association to a glass table, the analyst will note the complex propelling this fugue, but will gently bring the patient back to reacting specifically to the deal table.

To put it another way: the image, inherently, brings with it a set of constraints. An image cannot, by definition, have a boundless range of meanings. This is in direct opposition to the "Response as Reader" way of understanding material, where an image is the response the "reader" (in the case of literature) has to the image. The Jungian/orientational approach, on the other hand, while allowing for a wide range of subjective responses, requires that the responses be subject to the predetermined constraints that the image inevitably brings with it. In other words, subjectivity within an objective system of coordinates.

There is a nice Jewish story that perfectly illustrates this point. According to the Talmud, each paragraph of the Old Testament has 49 meanings. A rabbi asked his pupil studying the Old Testament to explain a certain paragraph. After the pupil finished, the Rabbi told him his explanation was wrong. "But," said the student, "according to the Talmud every paragraph has 49 meanings!" expostulated the aggrieved pupil. "Yes," replied the rabbi, "but yours is not one of them!"

For many people, this, at least initially, goes against the grain. This opposition is embedded very deeply in the culture. The deep assumptions of a culture are expressed in its language, and it is remarkable that the English language has difficulty with the issue of restraint. If we do not have the freedom to do anything we want, how do we describe the situation? I have used the term "constraint," the more common term is "limitation." But, unhappily, the term limitation has pejorative connotations. Who wants to be limited? Don't we all want to be free? "Boundaries," seems, at first glance, to be a better term, but, again, it is derived from the idea of to tie, bind, implying a negative restriction of freedom. I, therefore, use terms like a system of coordinates, a grid, matrix, or guidelines, which perhaps communicate best what I am trying to convey: namely, a set of rules the function of which is not to limit the activity, but, on the contrary, to guide it, make it possible. As in tennis, the court lines do not limit the game, they define it—there wouldn't be any game if not for the defining borders!

Boundaries are what give formlessness structure. We would be lost without them. In a particularly moving passage in Moby Dick, a crew member of the Pequod is thrown overboard in the middle of the ocean. When his absence is discovered after two days, the ship goes back for him, and when they find him, although he survived the ordeal, he has also gone mad—without guidelines to orient him, his ego disintegrated.

Appropriate boundaries play a crucial role in the analytic situation. For the analytic field to be properly constellated, two essential conditions have to be met: The first is absolute, hermetically sealed, confidentiality. The psyche of the analysand has to be convinced that whatever it comes up with will stay within the confines of the analytic process. If it has reasons to doubt the security of the container, it will have to manage the situation, ending up by filtering and selecting what is brought up. This is not necessarily a conscious process—the analysand's ego may trust the container (for instance, because they idolize the analyst), but if their psyche has grounds for caution, it will block the process. Thus, we find in subsequent analyses that in previous ones, large chunks of psychic material never made their appearance. Careful investigation shows that invariably the analysand's psyche did not experience itself as being in a secure place.

The second condition, which is not independent of the first, is that in analysis the analysand has the privilege, not found elsewhere in life, to say, feel, and image anything he or she wants without fear of the consequences.

It is clear that these two requirements necessitate the most solid of boundaries. Although this seems theoretically obvious, it is amazing how easily it is to breach. After all, the analytic encounter is between two human beings; an encounter, which by its very nature fosters a feeling of deep intimacy between the two participants. It is all too easy in the glow of this intimacy to try and break down the contrived structure of the analytic situation. The two people involved in the process would like to relate to each other as "human beings," rather than as a professional and a patient. The two participants are apt to do so for different reasons—the analysand because although they are in the analysis in order to know themselves, they are also, inevitably, afraid to encounter their truth. All analysands, consequently, try, in one way or another, to get the analyst away from the task at hand. The analyst, on the other hand, is frequently burdened by the projections cast on them and the expectations they have to carry. They would also like, from time to time, to stop being the analyst, and become a "regular" person, engaged in a deeply intimate relationship with another human being. When the two needs meet, there is collusion between analyst and analysand to turn away from the real task at hand, and the boundaries are broken. True analysis then ceases.

The physical arrangement of the classical Freudian analysis—the analysand lying on a couch with the analyst sitting behind them—has the advantage of stating very clearly that the analytic process is not an ordinary human encounter. In the Jungian creative dialogue, the two

The Analyst of My Dreams

participants usually sit face-to-face and engage in what may seem a normal conversation. In addition, from the very beginning, the Jungian endeavor consisted of trying to understand the material of the patient, which led easily to an overemphasis on the nature of the material, to the detriment of the interpersonal aspect of the relationship. Thus Jung was, to put it kindly, quite loose about his boundaries with his patients, and some of his followers have continued in this tradition.

Again, we owe a great debt to Robert Langs for raising the consciousness of the analytic community to the issue of boundaries. It is Langs' strong conviction that analysands come to analysis with an unconscious expectation of finding an archetypally (my term, not Langs') edenic, secure container. Any kind of ruffling of this idealized image, no matter how minuscule to start with, develops, very much in the fashion of chaos theory, into a major disruption. If the disruption is recognized in time and dealt with promptly, it can lead to important issues. But if the disruption has reached certain proportions, all is lost and the analysis destroyed. It is not humanly possible to maintain a paradisiacal container—after all, the analyst may become sick or go on vacation—but it is very important to try and strive toward one, and be acutely aware when the fragile fabric of the process is compromised.

Creating a safe container with proper boundaries implies, above all, establishing a sense of stability and reliability. The analytic hours should start on time, and end on time. A regular schedule has to be maintained. Adding or dropping hours in an erratic fashion should be avoided. At one time I was seeing a patient on a twice-a-week basis. After a while, a lot of material was coming up and the analysand requested switching to a three-times-a-week schedule. We spent the next 6 months exploring the nature of the fantasies that lay behind that request before we finally made the switch. We were changing the container, and we had to be sure that we were doing it for the right reason. Most analysts will spend a lot of time analyzing why a patient wants to reduce their hours; but, of course, increasing the number of sessions per week can be a subtle form of resistance as well.

Let us now turn to a fairy-tale which, in my opinion, illustrates the issue quite dramatically.

The Three Army Surgeons
Three army surgeons, who thought they knew their art perfectly, were traveling about the world, and they came to an inn where they wanted to pass the night. The host asked whence they came, and whither they were going. "We are roaming about the world and practicing our art." "Show me just once what you can do," said the host. The first said he would cut off his hand, and put it on again early next morning; the second said he would tear out his heart, and replace it next morning; the third said he would gouge out his eyes and heal them again next morning. "If you can do that," said the innkeeper, "you have learnt everything." They, however, had a salve, with which they rubbed themselves, which joined parts together, and they constantly carried with them the little bottle in which it was. Then they cut the hand, heart, and eyes from their bodies as they has said they would, and laid them all together on a plate, and gave it to the innkeeper. The innkeeper gave it to a servant-girl who was to set it in the cupboard, and take good care of it. Secretly, however, the girl had a lover who was a soldier. When everyone in the house was asleep the soldier came and wanted something to eat. The girl opened the cupboard and brought him some food, and in her love forgot to shut the cupboard door again: She seated herself at the table by her lover and they chatted away together. While she sat so contentedly there, thinking of no ill luck, the cat came creeping in, found the cupboard open, took the hand, heart, and eyes of the three army surgeons, and ran off with them. When the soldier had done eating, and the girl was taking the things and going to shut the cupboard, she saw that the plate which the innkeeper had given her to take care of was empty. Then she said in a fright to her lover: "Ah, miserable girl, what shall I do? The hand is gone, the heart, and the eyes are gone too, what will become of me in the morning?" "Be easy," said he, "I will help you out of your trouble—there is a thief hanging outside on the gallows, I will cut off his hand. Which hand was it?" "The right one." Then the girl gave him a sharp knife, and he went and cut the poor sinner's right hand off, and brought it to her. After this he caught the cat and gouged its eyes out, and now nothing but the heart was missing. "Have you not been slaughtering, and are not the dead pigs in the cellar?" said he. "Yes," said the girl. "That's fine," said the

soldier, and he went down and fetched a pig's heart. The girl placed all together on the plate, and put it in the cupboard.

In the morning when the three army surgeons got up, they told the girl she was to bring them the plate on which the hand, heart, and eyes were lying. Then she brought it out of the cupboard, and the first fixed the thief's hand on and smeared it with his salve, and it promptly grew to his arm. The second took the cat's eyes and put them in his own head. The third fixed the pig's heart from in the place where his own had been, and the innkeeper stood by, admired their skill, and said he had never yet seen such a thing as that done, and would sing their praises and recommend them to everyone. Then they paid their bill, and traveled farther.

As they were on their way, the one with the pig's heart did not stay with them at all, but wherever there was a corner he ran to it, and rooted about in it with his nose as pigs do. The others wanted to hold him back by the tail of his coat, but that did no good; he tore himself loose, and ran wherever the dirt was deepest. The second also behaved very strangely; he rubbed his eyes, and said to the others: "Comrades, what has happened? These are not my eyes! I don't see at all. Will one of you lead me, so that I do not fall?" Then with difficulty they traveled on till evening, when they reached another inn. They went into the bar together, and there at a table in the corner sat a rich man counting money. The one with the thief's hand went round about him, made a few jerky movements with his arm, and at last when the stranger turned away, snatched at the pile of money, and took a handful from it. One of them saw it, and said: "Comrade, what are you about? You must not steal—shame on you!" "Eh," said he, "but what can I do? My hand twitches, and I am forced to snatch things whether I will or not."

One of them said: "Things are not right with us, we have not got back again what is ours. We must return to the innkeeper, he has deceived us." They went back and told the innkeeper he better give them a great deal of money, otherwise they would set his roof on fire. He gave them what he had, and whatever he could raise. It was enough for the rest of their lives, but they would rather have had their own rightful organs.

This Grimm fairy-tale has many interesting themes in it, and may be approached in many ways. We should ask ourselves the following question: What is the real cause of the trouble in this story which causes things to go awry? We have to remember to be obedient to the orient of the fairy-tale, and respect the fact that fantastical things can happen in fairy-tales. So, the miraculous salve has to be accepted as given. It would also be erroneous, in my opinion, to focus on the boasting of the surgeons as the main cause of the trouble, and thus see this tale as a cautionary one about the folly of bragging of one's abilities. No, if we examine this tale meticulously, we have to come to the conclusion that the real trouble stems from the fact that the three organs were not stored properly—in other words, were not placed in a secure container. It seems to me that this tale, in its very allegorical way, directs our attention to the importance of the meticulous handling of the container. When we perform such profound operations, involving such crucial "organs" as the heart, eyes, and hand, as we surely do when a true analysis is conducted, we better make sure that the cupboard is securely locked and guarded, and not subject to the whims of the anima.

So we come to the crucial question: How do we assess clinically whether the analytic container is up to the task? First of all, we do all we can consciously to make it so, by virtue of what we have learned—by sticking to the appropriate rituals, and by adopting an analytic attitude. But as we know all too well, consciousness goes only so far. What if we are deluding ourselves? We may think we are maintaining proper boundaries, we may feel we are scrupulously obeying the guidelines of the material, but we may be mistaken. In any case, as we said before, we must have a provision for self-correction, a way that announces to us that the way we evaluate the situation is, in fact, incorrect.

There are several ways in which we can find out that we are misleading ourselves, but one of the most common and more potent ways is when patients bring us dreams that involve us, the analysts. These dreams, very often, throw into clear relief the nature of the true relationship between the analysand and the analyst, and express, in a truly objective way, an evaluation of the authentic relationship between the two people.

The Analyst of My Dreams

Let us take as an example the dream first mentioned in the introduction: An analysand dreams he is in a session with his analyst, except that the patient is sitting in the analyst's chair, and the analyst, in the patient's chair. From an orientational, objective point of view, the message is quite clear: The two participants have switched places! Due to whatever has been going on in the analysis, the psyche of the analysand is sending them both a message—it is now the analyst who has become the patient—he is the one who is benefiting from the analysis, not the one who legitimately ought to be benefiting from it. Imagine yourself the analyst getting a message like that! If you are an ethical person, you would have to inform your patient that your usefulness as an analyst to them has come to an end, and that they have now a higher level of consciousness. Not an easy thing to admit to, especially if pride is one of one's besetting sins. Not surprisingly, the analyst who published this dream did not see it this way. How did he get around it?

Freudians have defense mechanisms; Jungians have other means to get away from uncomfortable situations. The Jungian theory of dreams posits that one may look at dreams on two levels—the object level, and the subject level. The object level, which may also be called the interpersonal level, treats all figures and situations as referring to the actual people and situations in one's life. So, when a husband (or a wife) dreams about their mate, the dream should first and foremost be taken as making a comment on the actual marital situation. Thus, when a supervisee brings in a dream of a patient who has a recurring dream that her husband is suffocating her, it should be taken as a reflection of the actual marital situation. In her previous various analyses, these dreams were taken to point out to the analysand how her own animus is suffocating her.

This brings us to the second level of understanding: the subject level, which may also be called the internal level, in which all figures and situations are taken to represent partial inner aspects of the dreamer. Thus, the husband is seen as an animus figure. Theoretically, since dreams are produced by the psyche, in the ultimate sense, all dreams have a subject level interpretation, but as a matter of clinical practice, it is dangerous to bypass immediately the object level and shoot for the subject one—it is as if external reality does not exist, and is reminiscent of Freud's turning away from the possibility of all those incests taking place in real life to the conclusion that these were internal fantasies, thus changing forever the course of psychoanalysis.

Thus, dreams involving the analyst may refer to the two levels: On the object level, they would comment on the actual analytic situation, and, thus, would provide a possibility for self-correction; that is, that part of the methodology that permits the recognition of errors, omissions, and misunderstandings. It is instructive that Jung, in his examples where the dreamer dreams of him—for instance, a woman patient dreams she sees Jung sitting high above her, looking down on her—always takes the dreams on the object level, as referring actually to him; in this case, he had to face up to the fact that due to several circumstances he was, in effect, looking down on her, that is, being patronizing to her. At the other level, the subject level, the analyst represents the inner analyst, the inner guide, the emissary of the Self. In the chair switching dream example, the analyst opted to circumvent the painful object level interpretation, and, instead, concluded that what the dream indicated was that the analysis was progressing so smoothly that now the analysand was in a position to see the issues from the point of view of the analyst!

How are we to know whether to approach a dream involving the analyst from an object or subject view? This is, obviously, a crucial question. A very common dream, for instance, is one where the dreamer dreams they are in their analyst's office, when suddenly there is an intrusion by other people into the office, or other people are present in the session. Does that always necessarily mean that the analytic boundaries have been violated? It seems to me that it behooves the analyst first to explore this possibility in great depths; usually if the boundaries have been violated, the participants are not wholly ignorant of the fact, but may have chosen, by reasons of expediency, to ignore it. When I supervise trainees who bring me similar dreams, we nearly always find, rather easily, where the transgressions had occurred; in most cases the analyst had vague feelings of unease about them. In other words, they are not totally unconscious. These kinds of dreams are apt to appear in the beginning phase of the analysis, where the primary work is on the personal unconscious of the analysand.

The Analyst of My Dreams

Once we have a very evolved analysand, who has the general mapping of their personal unconscious, the map of their complexes, behind them, and the work on the more transpersonal level of their psyche is in process, then one can safely assume that the figure of the analyst in the dreams does, indeed, stand for the inner guide, the more evolved consciousness. One better be very sure of one's ground when dealing with this level, and be honest enough to be able to recognize when one is resorting to that level of understanding for the purpose of avoiding a painful truth. What would your reaction be if an analysand brought you recurrent dreams that you are feeding them ice cream, as an analysand of mine told me of dreams that he had had about his previous analyst?

It is very understandable why many analysts would chafe under this way of reading dreams. The consequences could be devastating. Let us take a look at a series of seven dreams, submitted by a woman analyst of a woman patient of hers. The submission was anonymous; I don't know who the analyst is.

- My analyst calls me on the phone to see how I am doing and to wish me good night. My sister overhears the conversation and ridicules my analyst's concern.
- I was with my analyst in a session. Her husband came into the room and interrupted us. Because of his taking so much time with her we didn't get our work done. I felt cheated, left out, not cared about. She doesn't appreciate what I have been through already. She has the answer for me and won't help me.
- My analyst is going to cut my time down. The implication is that I should shape up and get on with it. I'm very upset that she feels this way.
- I'm comforting my analyst. She shares her pain and growth that has arisen out of our work. She cries and I feel good about holding her.
- My analyst and I are in bed together. First she is on top and then I am on top. My analyst seems to be having an orgasm but I can tell it isn't real. I tell her that she doesn't have to fake an orgasm with me.

- I was having a session with my analyst in a kitchen. She put some food in front of me and went off to fix her own breakfast. It looked like a bunch of garbage and I was a little insulted. She was fixing the good stuff for herself. Then I noticed some bread and butter and a muffin in the garbage. I could make my own breakfast.

This series of dreams span seven years. God only knows what the analyst made of these dreams; clearly, by submitting them as an example of an analysis in which a development was occurring, she was indicating that in some mysterious way these dreams indicate some positive movement. From our discussion today, though, it should be clear that from an orientational point of view, these dreams spell nothing but a progressive disaster. Things go from bad to worse.

It starts in a mild enough way—the patient is called by her analyst at home. This, already, is an inappropriate action, and a strong violation of boundaries is indicated. The violation is elaborated in the second dream when the session is interrupted by the entrance of the analyst's husband. The patient's psyche is already sensing that the analyst's energy is elsewhere, and that the work is not getting done. The next dream indicates that the dreamer is experiencing her analyst as impatient with her, in other words, no true empathy. Then there is a role reversal; the sessions are about the pain of the analyst, and the dreamer is gratified by this. The mistreatment then takes the form of abuse, which takes a sexual shape. The dreamer is informed that the analyst is inauthentic, a faker. To sum it all up, the last dream tells us that what the analyst is feeding her patient is garbage. All in all, I find that a devastating commentary on the analyst and the analysis.

To be sure, not all dreams about the analyst are negative. In a good analysis the analyst very frequently appears in a supportive role. A very beautiful example—the analysand is a woman in her early fifties who is facing a very difficult health crisis, which, not unnaturally, has profound psychological implications for her. She has the following dream:

> I am among a group of people. We form a circle. I know this is my "healing circle." Your wife appears and joins the circle. Then you appear and you, too, join the healing circle. I am quite at peace.

The "you" in the dream refers, of course, to the analyst. This is a beautiful example of what can happen when the psyches of analysand and analyst work creatively and harmoniously together, as well as a beautiful example of the healing function of the psyche.

The circle is an archetypal (i.e., universal) symbol of wholeness. The *orient* of the circle is composed of at least two **dominants:** the circle as boundary, separating the outside of the circle and its inside, and the center, the focus of the circle.

An image (or a dream) can be understood on two levels: the *object level*, which refers to people and situations as they really exist in the outside world, and the *subject level*, in which everything is taken on an inner level: that is, people and situations represent parts of the psyche—aspects of the personality.

On the object level, the dream informs us that the actual relationship of the dreamer and her analyst is a crucial part of her healing process. On the subject level, it says that her inner analyst (and his counterpart, complementary aspect, represented by the wife, who, in reality is unknown to the analysand) is participating in a very active way in the healing.

The motif of integration and wholeness is repeated twice: first by the circle and second by the fact that both the analyst *and* his wife join the healing circle. It is an auspicious sign when a positive symbolic message is repeated twice, emphasizing its import.

All in all, the dream announces a potential for healing in this very difficult situation: a healing brought on by the actual relationship with the analyst, as well as the guidance of the inner analyst. From a scientific point of view, it sets up a testable hypothesis, namely that the analysand will, in time, emerge from her present, seemingly hopeless situation. The dream, like all dreams do not, as a rule, speak of a fait accompli, but of a potential. A lot of work will have to be done to turn the promise into reality. Here it took a year until full healing—both psychological and physical occurred.

Angels

IMAGES OF ANGELS ARE FAMILIAR TO US ALL. THEY ARE PRESENT IN MOST Western religious traditions and have even found their way into secular life. They are so much a part of our consciousness that we have woven them into our colloquial speech: We call someone "an angel" as a way of acknowledging an important service, as a way of saying "thank you." Major investors in theatrical productions are called angels. We all think we understand what an angel IS—a being who personifies goodness, who brings an important and beneficial message. However, a deeper understanding reveals something quite different and more complex.

In **The Way of the Image—The Orientational Approach to the Psyche**, I laid the groundwork for the translation of symbolic material into psychological language. I asserted that, in addition to the personal associations that are evoked by an image and that form the subjective level of our reactions to it, there is an objective stratum to the symbol, which goes to its essence. This objective dimension, which we termed the **orient** of the image, is the sum total of all the **dominants** (or **radicals**) that are inherent in it. In order to understand the orient of an image we have to have a deep knowledge of it, and to that purpose we can consult various reference books.

This methodology is straightforward enough when one deals with material reality; it is not that obvious when dealing with images that have a psychic reality, but not necessarily a material one. I would like to illustrate the application of the orientational approach to non-material images by trying to fathom the nature of angels. I am going to anchor the exploration of angels in a clinical example. This investigation will not only demonstrate the methodology, but will also serve, I hope, as a cautionary tale about the difference between approaching psychic material with precision, and dealing with it in a sloppy, imprecise way. The former can throw a clarifying light on a difficult case, guiding the analyst to a helpful and healing approach, whereas the latter is liable to mire the analysis in confusion and lead to an unfavorable clinical outcome.

Many years ago, in my first year as member of my professional association, a senior analyst threw down the gauntlet to an audience of analysts at a professional meeting. He presented a very difficult case that had stumped him and asked us for help. Unusually for a Jungian presentation, the analyst initially presented only one dream of the analysand: She was trying to cut a tree down with an axe. Prodded for additional dreams, the analyst responded that her dreams were mostly "insignificant." Asked for an example of such an "insignificant" dream, he gave the following dream:

There is an angel hovering between the earth and the sky.

The presenting analyst did not feel that the second dream was imparting any new, useful information. After all, all it was saying was that a messenger was hovering in the sky. The dream was not explicit, nor did it even seem to hint at what the nature of the message was; thus, it was not helpful.

The problem with this approach is the translation of the psychic image of an angel as a messenger. That is the traditional approach, and no wonder. There seems to be a good basis for it. The word angel comes from the Greek *angelos,* which means messenger. In itself it is the vulgate translation of the Hebrew *mal'ach,* also meaning messenger. Encyclopedias define angels as God's courtiers and messengers. In Zoroastrianism and the three monotheistic religions—Judaism, Christianity, and Islam—angels are taken to be "benevolent spiritual beings, powers or principles that mediate between the realm of the sacred and the profane realm of time, space, and cause and effect."

Angels play a crucial role in the theology of the aforementioned religions. In Zoroastrianism one of the *amesha spentas,* Vohu Manah (Good Mind) reveals to the Iranian prophet Zoroaster the nature of the true God. In Judaism, we have an angel wrestling with Jacob; a divine messenger tells Hagar that she will give birth to Ishmael; an angel restrains Abraham from sacrificing Isaac; the conception of Samson is announced to Manoah; the blessing of Jacob; Isaiah's vision of the seraphim; and in Daniel we have Michael and Gabriel. In Christianity, we have Gabriel going to Nazareth to announce to Mary that she is to be the mother of Jesus. In Islam, Gabriel reveals to Mohammed the nature of Allah and the Koran, and so on. Is it any wonder that the first impulse is to see angels as messengers? However, if we look more closely, we note that although in all those examples angels serve, indeed, as messengers, this does not tell us what their true nature really is, only what they happen to serve in those instances. American Indians have different kinds of messengers; so do African myths and folk tales.

How do we get at the very essence of angels? If we dealt with an object of the "real" world, we would reach for a reference book, a dictionary, or an encyclopedia to get a description of the significant properties of the object. If, instead of reaching for a partial, functional description of angels we turn to books of angels, we find a list of the various angels and their natures and responsibilities. Picking a few of them at random, we find:

Nathaniel:

Angel who rules fire, vengeance, and hidden things. He rules the sixth hour.

Dagiel:

Angel who rules over fish.

Harahel:

Angel who oversees libraries, archives, and rare cabinets.

Nuriel:

Angel of hailstorms and spellbinding power.

Omael:

Angel who governs chemistry and the perpetuation of species and races.

Pesagniyah:

Angel who takes the prayers of those in grief and deep sorrow and kisses them and then takes them to a higher place in heaven.

The one thing that strikes one immediately, of course, is that there isn't even a whiff of angels being messengers! What is common is that all these angels govern and hover over a territory. They are there before we approach the **territory**; they **precede** us. Therefore, we can say that: **Angels are confluences of established prevailing precedents.**

In other words, angels express the sum of all the qualities, assumptions, and meanings of what has come before.

Thus, an angel is a phenomenon of energy, a quantum of energy within space-time reality that exerts itself with real effect. When one says "the night came" and "the night was passed safely" there is an implication that some influence, some energic reality in that space-time saw to it that no lion ate one: There is a space-time energy seeing to it that one is in the right place at the right time, one has not been eaten by a lion while one is sleeping—that is the angel of the night. Anytime one approaches a point in space-time reality, one has to contend with the preceding prevailing energy system that hovers and governs over it. This energy system is **inherent** in the territory and was there **before** we arrived. Angels are like laws that govern a territory; we don't always know what the laws are, but they exist, and we must learn what they are if we are to prosper in that territory. This is much like a person coming to live in a new country and having to learn the laws and usages and language prevailing there. A contemporary example of an angel is a telephone system: It is an energy system governed by laws that precede us.

Angels

Enriched by this understanding, let us return to our clinical example. Now it is clear that the dream carries a very specific message to the analyst (this is one of those dreams that are directed primarily at the analyst—dreams are directed either primarily to the analysand, to the analyst or to the process), namely that the dreamer's task is to contend with an energy system that preceded her and that is hovering **between** heaven and earth. The clue to the specificity in dreams is very often in the unusual. One would expect the dreamer to say that there was an angel in the sky, but the dream says that the angel was between heaven and earth. Translated psychologically, the energy that she has to contend with is between the archetypal (heaven) and the personal (earth), that is to say, that which has preceded us in the world and connects a person to the archetypal world: the ancestral, or familial. This makes the previous dream, where she tries to fell the tree with an axe, quite clear—it is the family tree that she is trying to destroy! (Incidentally, this is another example of how dangerous it is to apply clichés to symbols. It would have been all too easy to fall into the error of thinking of the tree as her growth, or even her Self.)

In European aristocratic families it was quite common to have an ancestor with a dubious past, and the family was haunted by it. That was the case with our analysand, who was unconsciously living out an imitation of her ancestor. It could be predicted that if this situation is not handled with extreme precision and tact, the analysand would have a psychotic break; and, indeed, this is what happened to her. In the middle ages this situation would have been considered a possession and an exorcism by a priest would be prescribed, thus turning it into a spiritual matter.

Thus, ironically the angel has become a messenger after all; the message is that by getting to the very essence, to the core of an image, be it an image of this world or of the imagination, we get a set of very specific mandates and guidelines that serve to furnish us with a very precise map of the road we need to take, the royal road to the unconscious.

The Dreams of Gilgamesh as a Mythic Layer of the Psyche

*Gilgamesh was King of Uruk
A city set between the Tigris
And Euphrates rivers
In ancient Babylonia.
Enkidu was born on the Steppe
Where he grew up among the animals.
Gilgamesh was called a god and man.
It is the story
Of their becoming human together.*

Herbert Mason
Gilgamesh, A Verse Narrative

THE GILGAMESH EPIC, AN ANCIENT TEXT, PROBABLY FOUR OR FIVE thousand years old, is clearly a distillation of the wisdom of peoples from a very long time ago. Older than the Old or New Testaments, it has many versions and is probably a collection of versions. It appears in Ugric, Hittite, and Acadian texts, but we have not, by any means, come to the end of discovering the sources of this material. In many ways, the epic is a reflection of the myths that have sprung up all over the world in various forms.

Why do we need to study such mythical material? When we look around our world today, we can see the tremendous danger of the gates being flooded with the unconscious, and we see what the consequences are when there is no buffering or mediation by a conscious attitude toward this phenomenon. Studying mythical texts like the Gilgamesh epic is one way of providing a buffer, a consciousness, against the negative energy as it occurs in the collective culture, in the social awareness of people, and in our own lives.

So, how do we interpret myth from a psychological point of view? In dealing with symbolic material with a contemporary individual, we first hear about the person's life, about the context of that life. We ask that person for his or her reactions, associations, and amplifications. That is how we "situate" the image. What, however, do we do with ancient material? Obviously we can't ask the people who authored it to come and give us their associations. What we have to do is to situate that material in the context and culture of that time—in the psychological, geo-political issues that were then existent—and draw inferences from that. We have to rely less on the subjective element and more on the objective element. This was Jung's approach to myth, which differs from the traditional psychoanalytic approach that deals basically with the person's subjective reaction.

Every image in dream or myth can be applied on two levels. Of course, each image has infinite levels, but we seek the two primary levels. One is the internal level (the subjective level) in which all the figures and all the events are taken to be internal, in one person. Then there is the objective level (the interpersonal level) in which the symbols, the imagery, apply to the interactions between the person and the situations in which that person finds himself or herself.

What does Gilgamesh stand for from a psychological point of view? Gilgamesh is a king, a "big hero." He rules over the great state of Uruk, but he abuses his power. Inevitably, there is a rebellion by the populace. They raise their voices to the gods and ask that something be done to save them from this exaggerated form of kingship, of domination. The versions differ. Some versions claim that the rebellion of the people had to do with his exercising his droits de seigneur, of having his way with women. Others say that he subjugated the people in order to construct

The Dreams of Gilgamesh as a Mythic Layer of the Psyche 61

edifices for the glory of the city. Finally, the complaints reached heaven. The gods intervened and said, "We will send someone who will help to contain Gilgamesh." Aruru, the goddess of creation, who had created Gilgamesh in the first place, created a companion for him called Enkidu. The epic of Gilgamesh is essentially the story of Gilgamesh and Enkidu and the travail they went through.

It is very clear in the epic that there is much that is positive about Gilgamesh. He was very bright, very enterprising. But his strengths did not leave room for the individuality of others. What Gilgamesh stands for in us is the situation in which our strength becomes too one-sided. The cry of the populace to send someone to remedy the situation is, indeed, the earliest evidence we have of the urge to wholeness. At the very beginning, this myth informs us that the journey toward wholeness means balance and that there will be a rebellion of the system when a partial side, even though it may be a very worthy side, becomes exaggerated.

On the objective level "the system," which here rebels, refers to the culture or the family or the tribe. On the internal level, it is a part of the personality—the personality in its endosomatic capacity—that will rebel. Sometimes that happens in the body. The complaining populace can be taken, on the internal level, as some of the cells of the person when something is exaggerated or overused. Gilgamesh, from a Jungian point of view, may refer to the superior function, meaning the side of ourselves that we reflexively rely on. If we overuse that superior function, something comes from below to try to compensate for it.

Our culture encourages us to use the superior function. This is where our strength is. The culture says, "You are good at that; why don't you do that?" It does not say, "Why don't you try something else?" The Jungian definition indicates that neurosis is a compensation for one-sidedness. So, one can say that Enkidu was a neurosis that the system experienced due to one-sidedness.

When the neurosis appears, the first thing Gilgamesh does is to go to his mother. The mother, at that early level, is the "mater" or his very nature—the soma. Enkidu is made of the same "mater," but he is the result of the pleas of the people for help. The same god who created Gilgamesh is called upon to create Enkidu. Today, patients arrive at the analyst's office precisely because Enkidu has been created in them—but they don't know that.

We first meet Enkidu in the forest. He handles his whole life by instinct and, in fact, is identified with the instinct. He associates with the non-human at such a close level that he makes the human vulnerable. The Enkidu in us can exist at such an identification level that one doesn't even know it is there. It just takes over and makes you vulnerable, and it is not even aware of what it is doing. In the story, the people are instructed as to how they can make Enkidu more human so that he can then confront Gilgamesh and become his counterpart. They send what is called in one version "the harlot" to him. Of course, we are talking about a time when the harlot fulfilled a very different function from what the term "prostitute" means as used today. The harlot tames him.

We see here an interesting precedent to the motif of the Genesis story because the harlot is, of course, Eve. Before Eve (the harlot), a person is not conscious but is identified with instinct, as the people in paradise supposedly were before they ate from the Tree of Knowledge. What the harlot represents is that aspect of knowledge by which one becomes conscious of being a human being rather than an animal. Who you are and your objectivity now rely upon the maintenance of sufficient balance between the conscious and the unconscious. Or, to put it another way, although you are nourished by the unconscious, your conscious intention prevails. This is crucial and is one of the major themes of the whole Gilgamesh epic.

It does no good at all to interchange consciousness and the unconscious so that you end up consulting astrologers, throwing Tarot cards, and relying on non-rational elements. You are then abdicating your ego. By ego I do not mean the popular sense of vanity. I mean the center of consciousness, the agency in us that does the judging, the evaluating, the fielding.

It is very clear that what makes for a human being is the ability to take those forces that come from within, from the unconscious, and filter them through an ego, through a conscious capacity for differentiation. It is only by knowing the aspect to which you are totally vulnerable and upon which you are totally reliant that you are able to know who you are. Enkidu was totally vulnerable to the appeal of the harlot, and through her became humanized. Everyone of us must look inside and say, "What is the stuff in me that I am most vulnerable to?" It is this very stuff that allows you to really know yourself. Our culture is not very conducive to doing this because we are encouraged to think that what we are is what is strongest in us. And that is not so.

One of the amazing things about the Gilgamesh epic is that this early material contains such a plethora of dreams. It even offers various interpretations—the interpretation of the person listening to the dream and that of the person having the dream.

THE METEOR DREAM

In the first dream to be examined Gilgamesh tells Ninsun, his mother:

> "Mother, last night I had dream. I was full of joy. The young heroes were round me and I walked through the night under the stars of the firmament. And one, the meteor of the staff of Anu, fell down from heaven. I tried to lift it, but it proved too heavy. All the people of Uruk came around to see it. The common people jostled and the nobles thronged to kiss its feet and, to me, its attraction was as the love of a woman. They helped me. I braced my forehead and I raised it with thongs and brought it to you. You, yourself, pronounced it my brother."

This dream that precedes the creation of Enkidu shows that Gilgamesh has an intuition of what is about to happen. Psychologically, if one is in touch with the unconscious, one usually will have a glimmer of precognition before a major movement in one's life, whether this movement is created by oneself or happens to one.

How do we understand this from a mythical point of view? The emphasis here is upon the meteor, which is something coming from the sky. Therefore, we have to look at what the skies mean to humanity. What have we humans been doing with the skies? We have been projecting onto them. Projection, is a central concept of Jung and has to do with how the unconscious manifests itself. Both from the personal unconscious and the collective unconscious, we learn via projections. That is to say, we impute to external phenomena or people such things as are in ourselves, but with which we are not as yet in sufficient touch. From projection we learn about that to which we don't have sufficient access as yet. The more primitive one is, the more one tends to project, not recognizing that the projection comes from within, as well as, perhaps, being relevant to the outside.

Projection is not necessarily a defense mechanism although it can serve that way just as everything else can. Projection is, however, according to Jungian theory, the primary way through which we encounter the unconscious. It may be distorted but not necessarily so. If, for instance, I see your kindness and am moved by it, I am still projecting the kindness, even though you may truly be kind. But it is my kindness that I am projecting onto you. And, of course, it makes a vast difference whether or not the hook for the projection agrees with the projection. We tend to think of projections as always being untrue. But that is not Jung's idea.

Through all of recorded history, humanity has been projecting upon the skies, upon the stars. And, of course, we don't know whether the projections are correct or incorrect. In fact, the correctness of the projections may be meaningless. What is phenomenal is how consistent and reliable our projections have been. Over the centuries humanity has projected exactly the same thing on the stars and planets. It is the most constant, the most fixed, the most reliable screen for projection that we have had. I don't know of any other that has withstood the ravages of time as well as this particular projection.

So, when something comes from the sky, it means that a projection has fallen down. I think we all experienced this with the moon walk. After we saw moon-rise and earth-rise and saw people actually on the moon, consciousness experienced a change that we cannot reverse. In effect, in some ways, this moon-walk was a stunning validation of Jung's ideas because it showed that one could go and check out the projection without imploding it in the process.

The Gilgamesh epic describes a star or a meteor falling from the sky. (This is a very different thing from the UFOs that come not from the sky, but from another world, and that refer to something coming out of the collective unconscious.) In the Gilgamesh epic, it is a meteor, and it is the nature of the meteor to come down by burning itself out. So, the projection has burned itself out, and one can really come to terms with what lies behind it.

The meteors, as sky activities, are the relics of all the projections humans ever made. The projection isn't going to stay there forever and remain a stable guideline, but it falls to earth, becomes earth-born; this makes it very much a Christ-like symbol. And, as I said, because it is a meteor, it has "burned out" as a projection field and has become an earth-born reality.

THE AXE DREAM

The second dream comes that same night. Gilgamesh speaks again to his mother:

"Mother, I dream a second dream. In the streets of strong-walled Uruk, there lay an axe. The shape of it was strange, and the people thronged around. I saw it and was glad. I bent down. Deeply drawn toward it, I loved it like a woman, and wore it at my side."

The axe is an adaptive instrument—not for handling humans, but rather for handling the verdure of nature. It is a token-friend of the human condition. You may either call the thing that falls from the sky Enkidu, who becomes this extraordinary companion, or you may call it an axe. The axe is a cleaving instrument that starts the separatio, the process of separation. The axe was an instrument that allowed man to make further instruments. So the issue is, can one make anything that comes from heaven, such as Christ, one's life companion? The thing that comrades you is "other." To a man, the "other" is mostly woman, and the ultimate "other" is, of course, God.

THE FIRST MOUNTAIN DREAM

Then Enkidu and Gilgamesh start on a journey to conquer Humbaba, the evil giant of the forest.

> Gilgamesh and Enkidu pour meal upon the earth in order to gain the goodwill of the gods. This will persuade the gods to reveal their purpose through dreams. Our heroes lay down to sleep and after some time, Gilgamesh awakened his friend. "Enkidu, I have had a dream in which we were standing in a deep gorge beside a mountain. Compared to this mountain we were as tiny as flies. As we watched, the mountain collapsed and fell in a great heap." And Enkidu said, "Here is the meaning of the dream: Humbaba is the mountain, and he will fall before us."

There are quite a number of things here that are quite astounding. One important thing that happened is that Gilgamesh was not told of his destiny by God (by God appearing to him), but rather that he dreamed it. I find that extraordinary. As you know, in many times, in many cultures, and in many stories God appears to people and tells them what to do. But here, he comes via the dream! It is his own unconscious that informs him.

Here we see the beginning of internalization. And this raises the issue, unresolved to this very day: What is our role in our destiny? That is, perhaps, the crucial aspect of everybody's life, most certainly of anyone undergoing analysis: to be aware of the interplay between the hand that one is dealt (the divine guidelines that are part of one and about which, essentially, there is nothing one can do) and one's human reaction to them. This is what Erich Neumann called the Ego-Self axis.

In mythology, we find that the ego is represented by the human; the Self is represented by the divine. These two poles lead, of course, to problems of free will discussed by theologians and philosophers. It remains for us to determine, without hubris, without inflation, what it is one can and ought to do, and what it is that one must accept. We tend to fluctuate between the two.

Some people exaggerate what they can do, and they get into trouble because of that. Other people exaggerate their fate and become prey to superstitions and non-rational things without the interference and intervention of the ego. Still others succumb to a major depression due to the fact that they feel they can't really change certain things that, in fact, can be changed. And all of this is adumbrated by this mountain dream because that dream says: "This is your fate. You have to do it."

THE SECOND MOUNTAIN DREAM

Again they slept. After awhile, Gilgamesh again awakened his friend: I've had another dream, Enkidu. I saw the mountain again and suddenly it fell, and caught my feet from under me. Then an intolerable light blazed out. In the light was one whose beauty and grace were greater than the beauty of this world. He pulled me out from under the mountain: He gave me water to drink, and my heart was comforted. He set my feet upon the ground.

In the dream, the mountain stands for the most invincible territory. And that is a true crisis in life as well as in analysis. The very highest comes crashing down. The light is intolerable. Anyone who finds that life is tolerable is wasting the Gilgamesh experience. Here we have a warning: Life is, if genuine, intolerable to start with!

After these dreams, Enkidu is overcome by idleness. This is not necessarily the work of the devil but suggests idleness as a description of the non-use of the adaptive function. Enkidu is idle because he is not using his capacity for adaptation. And so, Gilgamesh decides, "Well, we still have tasks to perform."

There is that evil force in the forest called Humbaba, a very strong giant of immense proportions, that Gilgamesh and Enkidu are going to conquer. Here we find an interesting interplay between Enkidu and Gilgamesh. Enkidu tries, in the beginning, to dissuade Gilgamesh from undertaking such a perilous and hazardous journey. Gilgamesh responds saying, "I have to do this in order to leave my name for posterity. Even if I lose, I will have made a connection between my name and something that I have done. I will have put my name in the Book of Life." One must take responsibility for who one is and what one does. (Apparently at the time of this epic, one's name was still marvelously sacral.) Here we have the beginning of an "ego-like seed." It's the willingness to submit to one's own separateness from all other life. That is important. One must not get swallowed by the collective. It's better to fight Humbaba even if Gilgamesh loses. So, we are back to that ego statement that says (even in that early myth-forming period) that there is an instinct for knowing that every individual life counts if it does the thing it is required to do.

Gilgamesh goes first. And what does that mean? Psychologically, the "I will go forward" means I (the persona adaptation adjustment) will go first while you (the companion "conscience") will watch to determine if this is going right or whether I had better pull in my horns. What strikes us here is that while you are still identified with the persona of an action, you may not, in fact, be able to do the watching at the same time. Also introduced at this time is the issue of conscience which, from a Jungian point of view, has very little to do with Super Ego.

There are two aspects to awareness. First there is consciousness, which is the knowing. That is, of course, a *sine qua non*. First of all, you have to know. If you don't know, there is nothing you can do about it. But the knowing is only the first phase. Some people are very good at this, and they know a great deal about themselves. But then comes the far more difficult phase, the phase of conscience. This is the application of what you are conscious of, meaning that true knowledge has consequences.

A difficult point is reached when the individual must do something about his knowledge or understanding. Will he or she be willing to make the necessary sacrifice? The sacrifice may be small or it may be large. If you see that your behavior harms people you love, then once you become aware of it, what do you do about it? Do you continue to do the same thing saying, "Aha, now I know even better how to do this?" Or, does it bring you to a very painful and difficult readjustment in the way you deal with life and with the people around you?

Now comes a wonderful, wonderful thing in the story. When Gilgamesh announces his intention to go forward, Enkidu insists that Gilgamesh go and speak to Shamash, the Sun god, later called Samson. The implications here are staggering because one recognizes that one simply can't do the job of bringing about the wholeness without a profound rapport between the conscious and the unconscious and without going to the god. Then the god has, first, to agree and second, to provide essential help without which the journey cannot take place. (There are, of course, many parallels to that in various Greek myths where heroes get all kinds of shields and protective gear.)

I cannot overemphasize that this point is crucial for all of us. Suppose that one's personal requirement is to safely rearrange a complex that is destructive. Let's assume that the person, whether in analysis or in actual life, is heroically taking this on. Perhaps he may say, "I will stop drinking," or "I will stop tormenting my spouse or my children." Unless there are genuine dreams of an archetypal nature and/or unusual phenomena happening in his life, and unless there are genuine signs or symbols of an archetypal nature that the Self has, in fact, participated in creating some of the guidelines for this endeavor, the analyst, at least, knows that the endeavor will not prosper. And the analyst is wise to say to the analysand, "You can't do this. I, the companion so important to you, am going to dissuade you from doing this unless you 'talk to Shamash.'"

This is, of course, very frustrating to the beginning analyst who wants to change the world and who wants to improve everybody. Often, all the analyst can do is be a companion to the analysand. This is not, perhaps, as dramatic as working with someone who is able to change and improve and incorporate new things and get on with life in a wonderful way.

When one is not in analysis (after all, one can't very well be in analysis throughout all of life), one has to make that judgment for himself and ask, "Do I have what it takes—is it in me to be able to get out of the situation and overcome complexes that are destructive to me?" Some persons may discover, for instance, that they can't stop drinking on their own. They need AA, they need society, they need medication in order to do that. Some people have to deal with their "symptoms" and just be able to make meaning of it all. This is where Hillman's work is significant. He deals with how to "en-soul," how to make meaning of the stuff you cannot really change. And this is extremely hard to do without becoming prone to suicidal moods and very terrible "dark nights of the soul."

What happens next in the story is that Gilgamesh gets petulant with Shamash and says, "Look here, you planted the desire in me in the first place to go on this journey; you had better cough up the goodies for me to be able to do this." It is very easy to be misled by this issue. It is very easy to say to someone, "Well, since the issue has come up for you (in a dream), it means you can deal with it." Unhappily, sometimes the issue will come up in order for one to realize that it is not possible for him to deal with it—at least not in the anticipated way. Jung's **Answer to Job** illustrates that a cause-and-effect attitude in dealing with the divine is not productive or valid. Shamash gives Gilgamesh the strength (the winds, the tempest) and he gives him the full spectrum of the spirit, its shadow aspect (the tempest) as well as its positive side. Then Gilgamesh goes to his mother for advice and blessing. She puts on special clothes and all the paraphernalia of her queenliness. She does this in order that the advice will, in fact, be coming from the aspect of the Great Mother, the Gracious Mother, rather than from the personal mother. This also is the significance of the *Memorare* prayer in the Catholic Church. Here we see that the going to the mother is the going to the highest values one can go to in one's personal axis, to the anima, to the woman inside. And, as I said, whenever we deal with the mother, especially in the transpersonal, it also has something to do with "mater." It is going to the very matter of the person, the interface between psyche and soma.

THE BULL DREAM

Still on their journey, at the setting of the sun, Gilgamesh says, "Oh, mountain dwelling of the gods, bring me a favorable dream." Now, an analyst would smile at this request because to an analyst all dreams are favorable. In fact, as a rule of thumb, when a person says, "I had a terrible, frightening nightmare," I tell the person, "This is good news!" Conversely, if a person brings a wonderful dream, I say, "Watch out!" The reason for my response is, of course, that the unconscious comes to compensate. If the ego experiences what is coming as scary and terrifying, this is positive and normal. For example, if someone dreams he is being pursued and the pursuer is about to catch him, he wakes up with a thumping heart and is frightened. This is good news because the ego is about to confront an unknown aspect of the dreamer's self, and he should be frightened of something he doesn't know.

Gilgamesh asks for a marvelous dream and he gets one, though not, perhaps, the one he had expected:

> The sleep that the gods sent to me has broken. Ah, my friend, what a dream I have had! Terror and confusion! I seized hold of a wild bull in the wilderness. It bellowed and beat up the dust until the whole sky was dark. My arm was seized and my tongue bitten. I fell back on my knee, then someone refreshed me with water from his water jug.

So, you see, the favorable dream has to do with chaos and confusion, with an encounter with a very strong force. The encounter with the bull is the engagement with the nigredo, the worst part of the shadow. The wilderness stands for the territory that has not been maintained, contained, or made known; it is an uncharted course. When Gilgamesh falls back on his knee, we see that, even though it strikes him as unthinkable, he is forced to take a reverential position. Here we have the breaking of the hubris, which is necessary before the shadow can be assimilated. This is the required reverential attitude.

There are other dreams, and eventually Humbaba is conquered. But a very interesting thing happens. Humbaba pleads to be spared, and he offers to become Gilgamesh's servant. The fact that Humbaba was conquered, I think, is a wonderful intimation—an early indication that, under the right circumstances, raw instinct is no match for genuine ego consciousness. And that is really our main hope as the human race. But it is not an easy victory. Cunning is involved, not just raw strength. You can't just decide to do it. The decision is the first step, and this is where understanding, and ego consciousness, enter. The instincts ask to retain their present dynamic. They say, "Don't kill us; we will serve you." But if the instincts do retain their present dynamic, the ego will be destroyed. So Gilgamesh is warned by Enkidu that the dynamic of that instinct has to change. It has to suffer combative consciousness to find its true nature.

The story does not end here. Enkidu dies, and the heartbroken Gilgamesh goes in search of the everlasting life. The search fails, of course, and Gilgamesh is left to face his own mortality. Thus, the epic is full circle: from birth to death. It is a statement, expressed in ancient imagery and amazing dreams, about what constitutes a whole life, and some of the ways this wholeness comes about.

Notes and Sources

Notes
This article was transcribed by Joan Hagy Green from a taped lecture given at a meeting of The Round Table Associates for the Study of Jungian Psychology in 1994.

Sources
Herbert Mason, Gilgamesh, A Verse Narrative (Boston: Houghton Mifflin, 1971).

The dream texts are from The Epic of Gilgamesh, by N. K. Sandars (London: Penguin Books, 1960).

About the Author

Yoram Kaufmann, Ph.D., is a Jungian Analyst who originally trained as a physicist in his native Israel. Dr. Kaufmann earned his doctorate in Clinical Psychology from New York University. He has been on the faculty of the C.G. Jung Institute of New York, where he has also served as a member of the training board. His innovative work on the nature of the objective psyche has made important contributions to Jungian psychology as well as the overall vision of the Assisi Conferences. He maintains a private practice in New Jersey.